NEW DIRECTIONS FOR CO

Arthur M. Cohen
EDITOR-IN-CHIEF

Florence B. Brawer
ASSOCIATE EDITOR

Pam Schuetz
PUBLICATION COORDINATOR

Classification Systems for Two-Year Colleges

Alexander C. McCormick
The Carnegie Foundation for the Advancement of Teaching

Rebecca D. Cox
University of California, Berkeley

EDITORS

Number 122, Summer 2003

JOSSEY-BASS
San Francisco

CLASSIFICATION SYSTEMS FOR TWO-YEAR COLLEGES
Alexander C. McCormick, Rebecca D. Cox (eds.)
New Directions for Community Colleges, no. 122

Arthur M. Cohen, Editor-in-Chief
Florence B. Brawer, Associate Editor

Copyright © 2003 Wiley Periodicals, Inc., A Wiley Company. All rights reserved. No part of this publication may be reproduced, stored in a retrieval system, or transmitted in any form or by any means, electronic, mechanical, photocopying, recording, scanning, or otherwise, except as permitted under Sections 107 or 108 of the 1976 United States Copyright Act, without either the prior written permission of the Publisher or authorization through payment of the appropriate per-copy fee to the Copyright Clearance Center, 222 Rosewood Drive, Danvers, MA 01923, (978) 750-8400, fax (978) 750-4744. Requests to the Publisher for permission should be addressed to the Permissions Department, c/o John Wiley & Sons, Inc., 111 River St., Hoboken, NJ 07030; (201) 748-8789, fax (201) 748-6326, e-mail: permreq@wiley.com

New Directions for Community Colleges is indexed in Current Index to Journals in Education (ERIC).

Microfilm copies of issues and articles are available in 16mm and 35mm, as well as microfiche in 105mm, through University Microfilms Inc., 300 North Zeeb Road, Ann Arbor, Michigan 48106-1346.

ISSN 0194-3081 electronic ISSN 1536-0733

NEW DIRECTIONS FOR COMMUNITY COLLEGES is part of The Jossey-Bass Higher and Adult Education Series and is published quarterly by Wiley Subscription Services, Inc., A Wiley Company, at Jossey-Bass, 989 Market Street, San Francisco, California 94103-1741. Periodicals postage paid at San Francisco, California, and at additional mailing offices. POSTMASTER: Send address changes to New Directions for Community Colleges, Jossey-Bass, 989 Market Street, San Francisco, California 94103-1741.

SUBSCRIPTIONS cost $70.00 for individuals and $149.00 for institutions, agencies, and libraries. Prices subject to change.

EDITORIAL CORRESPONDENCE should be sent to the Editor-in-Chief, Arthur M. Cohen, at the ERIC Clearinghouse for Community Colleges, University of California, 3051 Moore Hall, Box 951521, Los Angeles, California 90095-1521. All manuscripts receive anonymous reviews by external referees.

Cover photograph © Rene Sheret, After Image, Los Angeles, California, 1990.

CONTENTS

Editors' Notes

The 2000 edition of the Carnegie Classification of Institutions of Higher Education lists nearly 1,700 public and private accredited, degree-granting institutions in its "Associate's Colleges" category (Carnegie Foundation for the Advancement of Teaching, 2001). (The list would be considerably longer if the degree-granting requirement were relaxed.) Unlike other major groupings, this very large and diverse group of institutions is not broken down into subcategories, nor has it ever been since the Carnegie Classification's initial publication in 1973. The Carnegie Classification was developed as a way to gain analytic purchase on the great diversity of U.S. institutions of higher education by creating categories of roughly comparable institutions. While its promise has largely been realized with respect to four-year institutions, as attested to by its wide adoption and endurance over three decades, the same cannot be said for the two-year sector. This volume is intended as a step toward addressing that need.

In the following pages, five different classification schemes are advanced and applied to a random sample of institutions for purposes of illustration and comparison. In addition, four contributors offer constructive criticism from three different perspectives: as representatives of a national association, as a seasoned community college educator and leader, and as a university-based researcher of two-year colleges. Although some of these schemes have been proposed previously, this is the first time that several distinct schemes have been presented together, applied to a common sample, and systematically critiqued from multiple perspectives.

We do not intend this to be the final word on classifying two-year colleges. Rather, we hope that it will serve to stimulate further discussion, critique, development, and refinement of approaches to the classification of this vital and diverse group of institutions. Indeed, we are encouraged by related work by other authors not represented in this volume, including dissertations by Milam (1995) and Johnson (1999), as well as a recent article on peer group identification by Hurley (2002).

In Chapter One, we elaborate the argument that classifying two-year colleges will contribute to the advancement of knowledge about these institutions while noting some of the unintended consequences that the Carnegie Classification has had among four-year institutions. This chapter also includes a brief conceptual discussion of classification approaches, and it makes the important distinction between classification and ranking. The last part of the chapter discusses some of the particular challenges in classifying two-year colleges.

Chapters Two through Six present the five different classification proposals. These examples testify to the difficulties involved in balancing the various purposes for which different audiences might employ a classification system. Thus the proposals are driven by distinct conceptions of how to define and differentiate two-year colleges. Despite these differences, four of the five approaches explicitly incorporate college size as one (and sometimes the only) classification criterion. The five chapters also differ in their definition of the universe of eligible institutions: two of the five include both public and private two-year colleges, while three confine their analyses to public colleges (in one case this restriction is due only to limitations in the available data). Four of the five proposed classification schemes are limited to degree-granting colleges; the fifth uses a broader definition that incorporates institutions that award only certificates. Finally, three of the schemes begin with prior conceptualization of the important differentiating factors and then move on to specific proposals, while two others take a more empirical approach, deriving their categories from patterns of similarity and difference revealed in the data.

Extending and elaborating his prior efforts to develop a classification for community colleges, Stephen Katsinas (Chapter Two) proposes categories that are fundamentally structural, taking several dimensions into consideration: control, characteristics of the surrounding community, size, specialization or distinctiveness of purpose, and administrative organization. He notes the importance of these factors in determining key differences in institutional function and operation. This approach seems particularly useful for policymakers at the state or national levels.

Gwyer Schuyler and Arthur Cohen both view differences in colleges' instructional missions as the fundamental organizing principle for a classification scheme. Drawing on a study of college curricula, Schuyler (Chapter Three) categorizes college missions by calculating the proportion of liberal arts courses (those offering traditional academic training and transfer to four-year institutions). Cohen (Chapter Four) likewise notes the significance of course offerings. Given the absence of national data, however, he advocates the use of total enrollment as a proxy for those patterns.

In Chapter Five, Jamie Merisotis and Jessica Shedd adapt their classification work conducted under the auspices of the National Center for Educations Statistics. Their approach uses empirical methods to find natural groupings of public and private two-year colleges.

While the role of student demand in shaping colleges is implicit in the work of Schuyler, Cohen, and Merisotis, Susan Shaman and Robert Zemsky (Chapter Six) apply an explicitly market-based framework in their empirically derived classification model. Using a multivariate analysis of price differences among community colleges, they extend their previous analyses of market segmentation among four-year colleges and universities to two-year colleges. This analysis leads them to find a fundamental (and somewhat surprising) consistency between the four-year market and the two-year one. Their results are then used to assign colleges to three distinct segments within the two-year market.

In the interest of enhancing the usefulness of this volume and stimulating further development and refinement of classification approaches, Chapters Seven through Nine offer reactions to the proposed classification approaches from several perspectives, each one representing potential classification users.

The contributors were asked to consider the following questions in assessing the various models:

Would the various schemes be useful to you in your work? How might they be improved?

Are there other important dimensions of variation that have not been addressed?

What unintended consequences might result from the adoption and proliferation of one or more of these classification schemes?

Applying their experience with the diverse constituency of the American Association of Community Colleges, Kent Phillippe and George Boggs (Chapter Seven) offer valuable feedback from a national policy perspective and set out important cautions about how classification might be misinterpreted and misused. Drawing on his extensive background as a community college educator and leader, Alfredo de los Santos (Chapter Eight) offers valuable insights into how the various models might be viewed from the campus or system perspective, with some cautions about temptations to make comparisons. Finally, Thomas Bailey (Chapter Nine) represents the research community, the constituency for whom the original Carnegie Classification was developed. His comments call attention to the need for more useful and comprehensive data describing the work of two-year colleges, and he illustrates the kind of data that, if available, would advance the cause of classification and thus the study of these institutions.

Chapter Ten reviews the practical application of the five proposed classification schemes, presenting the results of using each proposal to categorize an illustrative sample of two-year colleges. The chapter incorporates the results in the form of six exhibits. The first exhibit lists the colleges alphabetically, showing how each is classified according to the five schemes. The remaining exhibits show how each classification scheme groups these colleges, enabling readers to assess and compare the five proposals.

These classification schemes differ in their conceptualizations of both the meaningful distinctions among two-year colleges and the appropriate methodologies for bringing these differences into relief. While it is easy to criticize each scheme for what is overlooked or not included, an appreciation of the diversity of approaches and emphases calls attention to the need to match a chosen classification scheme to an analytic purpose. Each of these might be elaborated or improved on or may inspire still more novel approaches to defining and specifying important dimensions of variation among two-year colleges.

Alexander C. McCormick
Rebecca D. Cox
Editors

References

Carnegie Foundation for the Advancement of Teaching. *The Carnegie Classification of Institutions of Higher Education, 2000 Edition.* Menlo Park, Calif.: Carnegie Foundation for the Advancement of Teaching, 2001.

Hurley, R. G. "Identification and Assessment of Community College Peer Institution Selection Systems." *Community College Review,* 2002, *29*(4), 1–27.

Johnson, J. L. "A Study of Institutional Capacity and Financial Base at Rural Community Colleges." Unpublished doctoral dissertation, University of Toledo, 1999.

Milam, P. "Toward a Carnegie-Style Classification System for Publicly Controlled Community Colleges." Unpublished doctoral dissertation, Oklahoma State University, 1995.

ALEXANDER C. MCCORMICK is a senior scholar at The Carnegie Foundation for the Advancement of Teaching, where he directs the Carnegie Classification of Institutions of Higher Education.

REBECCA D. COX is a Ph.D. candidate in education at the University of California, Berkeley.

Part One

Classification Models for Two-Year Colleges

1

A credible and reliable classification system for two-year colleges will advance our understanding of this important sector of higher education. But developing such a system involves a number of challenges and may lead to unintended and largely unforeseeable consequences.

Classifying Two-Year Colleges: Purposes, Possibilities, and Pitfalls

Alexander C. McCormick, Rebecca D. Cox

In the early 1970s, the Carnegie Commission on Higher Education developed a taxonomy of colleges and universities to inform its research program. The resulting Classification of Institutions of Higher Education assigned every college and university in the United States to one of eighteen categories based on empirical data describing the institutions (for example, the type and number of degrees awarded, the range of fields represented or the concentration in a single field, the level of federal research funding, and admissions selectivity). The commission sought to make more manageable the complexity and variety of American higher education, creating groups of institutions that would be "relatively homogeneous with respect to the functions of the institutions as well as with respect to characteristics of students and faculty members" (Carnegie Commission on Higher Education, 1973). The Carnegie Classification has since been revised four times, most recently in 2000, to take account of institutional openings, closures, and mergers, as well as programmatic changes within institutions. In the three decades since its creation, the classification has proved to be a useful tool for researchers, policymakers, and institutional personnel interested in analyzing changes in the contours of the higher education system; analyzing the work, makeup, and activities of groups of institutions; and making sensible comparisons among institutions.

From the beginning, a shortcoming of the classification has been its failure to capture variation in the two-year sector of higher education. All two-year institutions have consistently been lumped together in a single category, despite their large and increasing representation both within the

Table 1.1. Carnegie Classification of Institutions of Higher Education, 1973 and 2000

	Number of Institutions		*Percentage of Total*	
Year	*1973*	*2000*	*1973*	*2000*
Total	2,837	3,941	100	100
Doctorate-Granting Universities				
Research I and II (1973), Doctoral/Research Extensive (2000)	92	151	3.2	3.8
Doctoral I and II (1973), Doctoral/Research Intensive (2000)	81	110	2.9	2.8
Comprehensive or Master's Universities				
Comprehensive I (1973), Master's I (2000)	323	496	11.4	12.6
Comprehensive II (1973), Master's II (2000)	133	115	4.7	2.9
Liberal Arts or Baccalaureate Colleges				
Liberal Arts I (1973), Baccalaureate-Liberal Arts (2000)	146	228	5.1	5.8
Liberal Arts II (1973), Baccalaureate-General and Baccalaureate/Associate's (2000)	575	378	20.3	9.6
Two-Year Colleges (1973), Associate's Colleges (2000)	1,063	1,669	37.5	42.3
Specialized Institutions	424	766	14.9	19.4
Tribal Colleges (2000 only)	N.A.	28	N.A.	0.7

Source: Adapted from McCormick, 2001, tab. 5.

universe of institutions (38 percent in 1973, 42 percent in 2000) and in terms of the proportion of enrolled students (28 percent in 1973, 40 percent in 2000); see Table 1.1 (Carnegie Commission on Higher Education, 1973; Carnegie Foundation for the Advancement of Teaching, 2001). Indeed, in the 2000 edition, the single category containing all two-year colleges contains more institutions (nearly 1,700) than the seven groupings used to differentiate doctorate-granting, master's (or comprehensive), and baccalaureate colleges combined. This shortcoming of the classification is somewhat understandable. A fundamental organizing principle for the classification is an institution's degree offerings, and many category distinctions are based on the record of degree conferrals. The conferral data include information about corresponding fields of study, permitting further differentiation with respect to disciplinary breadth or concentration. Thus, for example, baccalaureate colleges are distinguished with respect to the proportion of graduates majoring in liberal arts fields. But a focus on degrees (or certificates) is not nearly as useful for classifying two-year colleges because much of their work is not oriented to formal credentialing. A classification of community colleges based on the record of degrees or certificates would therefore be of questionable value.

Nevertheless, given the diversity of two-year colleges, it seems certain that a credible and reliable classification scheme will help advance our understanding of this vital group of institutions, much as the Carnegie Classification has contributed to research and practice with respect to four-year colleges and universities. It is the intent of this volume to stimulate the development and application of such classification schemes.

The Purpose of Classification

Two definitions help frame the discussion of what we mean by classification:

class: a group, set, or kind sharing common attributes
classification: systematic arrangement in groups or categories according to established criteria

In his useful volume on classification techniques in the social sciences, Bailey defines classification simply as "the ordering of entities into groups or classes on the basis of their similarity" (1994, p. 1).

The aim of classifying two-year colleges is simple: to identify categories of institutions that share common characteristics, in the interest of advancing knowledge about this important sector of higher education. A valid classification scheme would provide interested groups (researchers, policy analysts, institutional personnel) with a convenient, easy-to-use, and widely understood way to grapple with the diversity of this institutional sector.

Classification is distinct from ranking. The intent of classifying colleges is not to make quality judgments or to induce ambitions for colleges to change categories. This has been a thorny issue for the Carnegie Classification among four-year institutions, as particular categories are sometimes thought to imply institutional quality or status. Certain aspects of its structure have contributed to this confusion of classification and ranking: it has traditionally used the Roman numerals I and II to make distinctions within major groupings (doctorate-granting, master's, and baccalaureate); many nationally known and highly regarded institutions are classified together, typically in the first listed subcategory of research universities or baccalaureate colleges (denoted by Roman numeral I), reinforcing the interpretation that the categories differentiate with respect to quality; and some people feel that the very order in which categories have been presented implies a judgment about quality or importance. This history offers important lessons to anyone seeking to categorize or classify colleges and universities: inappropriate or improper interpretation and usage cannot necessarily be foreseen, nor can they be prevented. But an awareness of this history can also constructively inform the creation of any new classification scheme.

Conceptual and Methodological Considerations

There are different ways to develop a classification scheme. One approach begins with a theoretical or conceptual understanding of the major categories to which entities shall be assigned and then seeks empirical criteria that can be used to assign entities to these conceptually defined categories. (This is the approach that led to the current Carnegie Classification system.)

Alternatively, one can begin with a list of variables thought to differentiate entities in important ways—the selection of which rests on some degree of theoretical or conceptual understanding, whether explicitly stated or not—and then use a statistical procedure such as cluster analysis to create categories that minimize within-group differences with respect to these variables while maximizing between-group differences. In either approach, the resulting categories are both mutually exclusive and collectively exhaustive: every entity is assigned to a category and to only one category (Bailey, 1994).

Both approaches are legitimate, and to some degree the choice depends on the state of knowledge development with respect to the subject of classification. The first approach depends on a well-developed and comprehensive understanding of the phenomenon of interest, to guide the conceptual delineation of categories as well as the search for appropriate empirical criteria that will be used to define the categories. Thus conceptually derived classifications are more common in mature fields, in which a comprehensive body of literature and research can inform classification development (Kwasnik, 1999). The second approach is more exploratory, requiring no a priori expectation of what appropriate and meaningful categories would be: rather, the categories emerge from the analysis of similarity and difference with respect to the chosen variables. This calls attention to the importance of selecting the right variables to guide an empirically derived classification.

Simplification is an important goal of classification: complex patterns of variation are distilled into a finite set of categories that reduce cognitive burden while capturing and representing meaningful variation. This suggests a critical trade-off that the classifier confronts in choosing how finely to differentiate (that is, in choosing the number of distinct categories in the classification scheme). An interest in precise description and relative homogeneity within categories drives up the number of categories, while an interest in parsimony calls for fewer categories at the cost of greater within-group variation. Analytic usefulness is also an important consideration related to the number of categories: each one should contain a sufficient number of entities to support the ensuing uses of the classification (such as comparing categories on a set of criterion measures).

Specific Issues in Classifying Two-Year Colleges

We have just contrasted two different approaches to deriving a classification system, one conceptually driven and the other empirically driven. Both approaches require data. In a classification exercise such as the one contemplated here, in which the ambition is to classify every institution, the availability of appropriate data, or the feasibility of collecting data that are required but not available, amounts to a very significant constraint on what can be accomplished. Indeed, as suggested earlier, it is likely that the Carnegie Classification's failure to differentiate two-year colleges is attributable at least in part to shortcomings in the available data. But setting aside this constraint for the moment, we consider a range of other issues that will need to be taken into account in developing a useful classification system. These include inevitable comparisons with four-year institutions, the range of possible users or audiences, the variety of missions served, differences related to institutional control, and differences in administrative organization and funding.

Creating a classification of two-year colleges involves many challenges. For the system to serve as a useful tool while maintaining a descriptive rather than evaluative character requires careful consideration of a range of issues, which this volume only begins to explore. The difficulty lies, in part, in the status of the two-year college. Any comparison—express or implied—in which the four-year model represents the standard necessarily relegates the two-year sector to a lower tier. Conceiving of appropriate descriptive categories is indeed a delicate task. For this reason, considering the landscape of two-year colleges in isolation from other colleges and universities is a valuable exercise, serving to illuminate the key contours of the sector without judgment about where it falls short of the traditional college model. At the same time, two-year colleges *are* part of the larger universe of colleges and universities. The categories applied to the two-year sector may thus have relevance to the larger classification project. An issue to consider, then, is the extent to which elements of the two-year classification are relevant and meaningful for other institutions and whether (or how) the two-year classification scheme might enable new forms of cross-sector comparison.

Another substantial challenge inheres in the audience and users of the new system. The diverse agendas of different stakeholders—academic researchers, policymakers, college personnel, students, and members of various other constituencies and associations—promise an equally diverse set of objectives in using a classification. In the case of regional- and state-level policy, for example, the national concern with assessing the efficiency of colleges' performance increases the likelihood that the relevant categories will be scrutinized for such accountability purposes. Furthermore, the preferences of each distinct audience may differ on many counts—from informational content to level of specificity. Thus while the fundamental features of two-year colleges could be delineated with a single system, the range of possible users suggests the advantage of a more flexible (and complicated) scheme or a set of distinct schemes corresponding to different audiences and different uses.

Addressing the multiple audiences of the two-year college classification is only the first of many complicated issues. Fundamentally, many of the dilemmas in describing the community college sector emerge from the multiple missions that it fulfills. Several core community college offerings, such as courses that earn transfer credits to four-year colleges and remedial coursework for inadequately prepared students, correspond to activities that occur at the four-year level. Other functions, such as the provision of credit-bearing courses in technical occupations or the vast array of noncredit educational offerings, do not play a central role in the traditional conception of the four-year college mission.

Colleges vary in the extent to which they serve these distinct functions, and describing colleges' involvement in these areas constitutes one possible basis for classification. Defining these functions in distinct categories, however, is not entirely straightforward. The conventional distinction within the credit program offerings, between academic courses (alternatively labeled liberal arts or transfer-level courses) and occupational courses, no longer comprises mutually exclusive categories. For example, certain occupational programs, in areas such as nursing, information technology, and accounting, lead to specific work skills and certifications and are also eligible for transfer credit toward a bachelor's degree program. Similarly, individual courses may integrate both academic and occupational content, carrying transferable credits while developing workplace knowledge and skills. Perhaps this is an opportunity to redefine the functional categories across all sectors of higher education, employing vocabulary that clarifies community colleges' role in professional career preparation as well as their contributions to technical career training. Employing more precise vocabulary, however, does not resolve the complications associated with the variable status of distinct educational missions.

The area of basic skills coursework provides a clear illustration. As public four-year colleges in many states attempt to limit their participation in remediation, the provision of remedial coursework at two-year colleges carries greater policy implications. The nature of a college's involvement in remediation is integrally related to state policy at the secondary and postsecondary levels. Nonetheless, the extent of a college's remedial activity can easily be misconstrued as an indicator of the quality of instruction. Thus comparisons across colleges can become a basis for improper and misleading evaluative judgments. And while the designers of a classification system cannot ensure its proper use, certain areas of ongoing controversy deserve a cautious approach. Areas of concern, such as degree completion rates or the proportion of adjunct faculty, constitute perilous territory where the classification system could easily foster simplistic and misguided assessments of value, quality, and effectiveness.

In the case of credentialing, because students' paths through community colleges do not necessarily culminate in a degree or certification, delineating the multiplicity of educational offerings provides one way to recognize the flexibility that exists beyond the traditional college-going model. Current economic realities require many students to pursue work and school simultaneously. An educational path may include periods of stopping out and then returning to college, and indeed it may combine attendance spells at many colleges (McCormick, 1997; Adelman, 1999). Likewise, individuals in the workforce are unlikely to experience an uninterrupted ascent on a single career path. That nearly 10 percent of credit-bearing community college courses are taken by students who have already earned a bachelor's degree is testimony to the variety of educational paths served by the two-year sector (Quinley and Quinley, 1998).

In view of the expanding patterns of college-going activity, a classification of higher education institutions demands a clear and comprehensive definition of the landscape. The universe of two-year colleges consists of both public and private colleges, including an increasing proportion of proprietary colleges. It seems arbitrary, then, to limit the classification to public community colleges. This points to two distinct questions: Are there meaningful comparisons to be made among these distinct two-year institutions? And what are the implications of including (or excluding) private institutions of either kind from the classification system? Functional differences exist between public and private not-for-profit colleges, on the one hand, and proprietary colleges, on the other. Features typical of proprietary colleges, such as highly specialized and targeted services, selective admission requirements, and higher tuition, complicate the utility and sensibility of comparing them with other colleges. But both forms of private colleges are clearly part of the market for postsecondary education, and they compete with public community colleges for the same students. Indeed, in a comprehensive classification of two-year colleges, it would make sense to include institutional control among the criteria used to distinguish categories.

With respect to administrative structures and their influence on colleges' internal functioning, the more comprehensive two-year colleges present an additional set of difficulties. First, administrative functioning in a single-college district is considerably different from that in a centrally managed district with multiple colleges. Second, while the internal governance and funding structures are shaped by state-level policies, community colleges are highly responsive to their locale, forging partnerships with local businesses, developing activities in response to local economic conditions, and serving other community needs. Thus a series of interrelated factors influences the work that occurs within two-year colleges, including regional location, size, population density, and income level of the service district. Finally, although the local tax base may have a significant impact on a college's financial affairs, the funding picture is incomplete without taking into account the full range of funding sources and the proportion of support from each source.

Conclusion

There are ample reasons to believe that one or more new systems for classifying two-year colleges will be a valuable step in the advancement of knowledge about these institutions and will be useful to researchers, policymakers, and college personnel. But the development of such classification schemes faces a number of challenges related to the availability of appropriate data on which to make classification decisions and more importantly on the large number of dimensions along which variation exists.

We have noted that a new classification might lead to improper judgments about such matters as quality and productivity. We should also return to the lessons about unintended consequences taught by the experience of four-year institutions with the Carnegie Classification. The most nettlesome of these consequences—at least from the standpoint of the organization responsible for the classification—is the extent to which it is seen by many as a ranking system, which has led in turn to explicit institutional ambitions and strategic action to change categories to "move up." (An important distinction needs to be drawn here: there is nothing wrong with movement within the Carnegie Classification as long as it is a consequence of, and secondary to, mission-driven changes. The objection is to change that is undertaken explicitly, if not exclusively, in the interest of obtaining a change in classification.) To the extent that the naming of categories has caused or reinforced interpretations that the categories represent judgments about quality, this problem can largely be avoided through the judicious choice of terminology and presentation. But as noted earlier, the rankings inference is also likely due to the clustering of high-status institutions in certain categories. Here the differences in the organizational ecologies of two- and four-year institutions may mitigate the problem. Two-year colleges do not compete in a national market in the way that four-year institutions do (or aspire to). Thus the stakes of classification are considerably lower, and it seems unlikely that a given college would seek to change categories in order to benefit from affiliation with a particular set of prestigious two-year colleges. Thus we may hope that appropriate and meaningful approaches to classifying two-year colleges will bring positive benefits of analytic utility for college personnel, policymakers, and researchers without the adverse consequences associated with misguided inferences about ranking and hierarchy.

References

Adelman, C. *Answers in the Tool Box: Academic Intensity, Attendance Patterns, and Bachelor's Degree Attainment.* Washington, D.C.: Office of Educational Research and Improvement, U.S. Department of Education, 1999.

Bailey, K. D. *Typologies and Taxonomies: An Introduction to Classification Techniques.* Thousand Oaks, Calif.: Sage, 1994.

Carnegie Commission on Higher Education. *A Classification of Institutions of Higher Education.* Berkeley, Calif.: Carnegie Commission on Higher Education, 1973.

Carnegie Foundation for the Advancement of Teaching. *The Carnegie Classification of Institutions of Higher Education, 2000 Edition.* Menlo Park, Calif.: Carnegie Foundation for the Advancement of Teaching, 2001.

Kwasnik, B. H. "The Role of Classification in Knowledge Representation and Discovery." *Library Trends,* 1999, *48*(1), 22–47.

McCormick, A. C. *Transfer Behavior Among Beginning Postsecondary Students, 1989–94.* Washington, D.C.: National Center for Education Statistics, U.S. Department of Education, 1997.

McCormick, A. C. "The 2000 Carnegie Classification: Background and Description." In Carnegie Foundation for the Advancement of Teaching, *The Carnegie Classification of Institutions of Higher Education, 2000 Edition.* Menlo Park, Calif.: Carnegie Foundation for the Advancement of Teaching, 2001.

Quinley, J. W., and Quinley, M. P. "Four-Year Graduates Attending Community Colleges: A New Meaning for the Term 'Second Chance.'" Community College Research Center paper, August 1998. Retrieved January 26, 2003, from [http://www.tc.columbia.edu/~iee/ccrc/public.htm].

ALEXANDER C. MCCORMICK is a senior scholar at The Carnegie Foundation for the Advancement of Teaching, where he directs the Carnegie Classification of Institutions of Higher Education.

REBECCA D. COX is a Ph.D. candidate in education at the University of California, Berkeley.

2

In this chapter, the author proposes a classification scheme based on institutional control, geography, governance, and size in order to capture the diversity of two-year colleges in the United States.

Two-Year College Classifications Based on Institutional Control, Geography, Governance, and Size

Stephen G. Katsinas

> We need an architecture that recognizes the diversity of these institutions.
>
> —Ken Kempner, American Association of Community Colleges Symposium, 1993

My journey into classifications began in 1990 when as a new assistant professor of higher education I became increasingly frustrated with the low response rates of community college practitioners to my students' dissertation surveys. With response rates typically at or below 50 percent, well below that of other fields in my college of education, my colleagues often concluded that the quality of community college–oriented research was low. This in turn had a carryover effect that lowered the perceived value of my own research. Later I learned that community college scholars at other universities shared this problem. In his 1996 address as president of the Association for the Study of Higher Education, Patrick Terenzini cited the lack of good empirical research on community colleges as one of the three great holes in the higher education research literature.

No generally recognizable method for drawing representative samples for community colleges existed. This situation was very different from that of other types of institutions of higher education, which relied on the widely accepted Carnegie classification scheme. Surveys of community colleges had

---

The author wishes to acknowledge past support from the Ford Foundation.

to be administered to either the entire universe of community colleges nationwide or by regions or states. Researchers had to accept whatever "noise" was inherent in such an approach. The practical result, however, was that community college presidents came to be literally besieged by surveys. So prevalent are surveys that the American Association of Community College (AACC) markets on its Web site the purchase of mailing labels for member CEOs specifically for dissertation students. Many CEOs, particularly at smaller institutions, choose not to respond at all.

So where to start? I first spoke to two giants in the field of community college scholarship, the late S. V. "Marty" Martorana and Raymond J. Young, who between them provided consulting services to establish hundreds of community colleges across the nation between 1950 and 1975. Both indicated that a classification scheme was badly needed and that the task would be very difficult due to the diversity among two-year institutions and state systems. Recognizing the daunting task that lay ahead, I developed a paper in 1993 for what is now called the Council for the Study of Community Colleges and soon received a small grant from the Ford Foundation to begin basic research on developing a classification scheme for community colleges.

This chapter describes the development of an inclusive, easily accessible methodology for practitioners, state and federal policymakers, and researchers using objective criteria to classify two-year institutions. The criteria include institutional control for public, private, and special-use or federally chartered institutions. Further classification within the public sector is made on the basis of geography (rural, suburban, or urban); in the public suburban and urban subcategories, the type of governance (multicampus or single campus); and in the public rural subcategory, enrollment size (large or small). The goal is to capture the diversity of two-year institutions across America making it easier for researchers to draw representative survey samples and to make effective use of existing federal data sets. We will first examine the uses of classifications and then look more closely at the classification criteria.

Uses of Classifications

The higher education literature implicitly assumes great homogeneity among community colleges in terms of state-assigned mission and functions, organizational complexity, finances, and students served. The notion of homogeneity was reinforced by the classification scheme developed by Clark Kerr in the 1970s, maintained since that time by the Carnegie Foundation for the Advancement of Teaching. The reality, however, is very different. While sharing a commitment to open access, comprehensiveness, and responsiveness to local needs, two-year colleges in America are in fact quite diverse in terms of institutional control, geography, governance, and size. These differences are reflected by the roles played by college actors at all levels of the organization (Katsinas, 1996).

Two-year college practitioners as well as regional accrediting organizations and state policymakers are aware of these differences (Katsinas, 1993, 1996). Type of control, geography, governance, and size are included in virtually every executive-level job advertisement carried in *Community College Times, Community College Week,* and the *Chronicle of Higher Education.* Trustees and search consultants seek candidates who can function within the college's specific region or community. Experienced candidates implicitly know that the management knowledge and personal leadership style required to administer a rural, single-campus community college is much different from that needed to govern a large, multicampus urban district (Bowen and Muller, 1999).

The usefulness of classification to practitioners, policymakers, and researchers is tied to whether or not it meaningfully captures reality. Put simply, classifications help frame how we know what we know. Practitioners can greatly benefit from an agreed classification scheme that provides institutional comparisons to assist in creating benchmarks to assess and improve educational practice. For example, transfer is recognized as an important function of the community college. Arthur Cohen (1994) has documented the relative stability of institutional transfer rates over time. In a number of presentations, he has summarized his findings by saying, "Institutions that are good at transfer are good at transfer," meaning that community colleges with good transfer rates work to ensure that their internal academic and student support services reinforce teaching activities that promote transfer. Cohen's research suggests that the process of increasing transfer rates is a deliberate one. However, more information than transfer rates is needed to make meaningful institutional comparisons.

Consider the case of two similarly sized cities in Ohio, Dayton and Toledo, which are served by Sinclair Community College and Owens Community College, respectively. At first glance, a new state legislator might assume that both institutions are similar in their funding. However, Sinclair students pay $834 per year in tuition and fees, while Owens students pay $2,040 each year. Sinclair receives roughly $20.8 million each year from local property taxes (personal communication, Budget Office, Sinclair Community College, May 13, 2002), while Owens receives no local tax support at all. Can there be any question as to which institution would have more in the way of updated technology, student and academic support services, and professional development opportunities for faculty and staff that might promote expanded transfer? To take the example one step further, at which institution will the federal and state student direct grant aid programs designed to promote access go farther? Without the existence of a good classification scheme, intrastate comparisons by state policymakers can result in unintended harm.

The new Baldrige quality accreditation process used by leading regional accreditors such as the North Central and Southern Associations of Colleges and Schools requires identification of peer institutions for benchmarking purposes. Data on a wide variety of practices and outcomes are typically collected and shared, including student retention, budgeting, transfer, and faculty development. For benchmarking to work, smaller community colleges in rural settings and large multicampus urban districts must be grouped with similar institutions. If one accepts the notion that benchmarking helps the accrediting process improve institutional practice, which in turn benefits faculty, staff, state policymakers, taxpayers, and most important of all, students, then classifications are indeed important.

Community college practitioners and professors of higher education engaged in graduate education for community college leaders know well the striking differences between urban multicampus and rural single-campus community colleges. Researchers from outside the field, however, including economists, political scientists, and sociologists, do not know and cannot be expected to make such distinctions. A classification system should assist the broad research and public policy community to examine access and equity issues raised by such discrepancies in a world of increased devolution in related programs that include welfare-to-work, adult literacy, and job training.

Some General Principles in Classifying Two-Year Colleges

Table 2.1 describes the proposed classification scheme developed by Vincent A. Lacey of Southern Illinois University and myself. Our goal was to develop a Carnegie-style classification scheme for community colleges. We identified three key factors that helped Kerr's classification scheme become widely accepted by the research and public policy communities. First, Kerr and his successors used objective data from nationally recognized sources. Second, the criteria were generally recognized as meaningful by users, specifically the number and level of degrees awarded (doctoral, master's, baccalaureate, associate), which largely mirrored the organization of the nation's largest public system of higher education, that of California. Third, the major classification groupings proved to be fairly stable. These factors made the Carnegie classification system relatively easy to use over a long period of time by various user communities.

Like Kerr's original scheme, the classification of two-year institutions presented in Table 2.1 uses objective data. These data include institutional control (public, private, or federally chartered and special-use institutions) and, within the public sector, geography, governance, and size. The data are from the 1993 Integrated Postsecondary Education Data System (IPEDS) Institutional Characteristics data file. (As of this writing, we are updating our classifications using the 2000 census and 2000 IPEDS data files.) The intent is to create an *inclusive* classification system of two-year colleges that is both *stable* and *meaningful* to practitioners, researchers,

Table 2.1. A Classification System for Community Colleges

	Number of Institutions	*Number of Students Served*
I. Publicly Controlled Two-Year Institutions	1,070	5,509,280
A. Rural Community Colleges	736	1,773,066
1. Small colleges (under 2,499 students)	461	542,315
2. Large colleges (2,500 students and more)	275	1,230,751
B. Suburban Community Colleges	211	1,920,034
1. Single-campus	171	1,196,073
2. Multicampus	40	723,961
C. Urban Community Colleges	123	1,816,180
1. Single-campus	65	417,744
2. Multicampus	58	1,398,436
II. Privately Controlled Two-Year Institutions	836	338,195
A. Private nonprofit	116	73,179
B. Proprietary	720	265,016
III. Federally Chartered and Special-Use Institutions	595	133,544
A. Tribal colleges	29	13,938
B. Special-use institutions	566	119,606
Total, all institutions	2,501	5,981,019

Notes: Institutions were classified using data from the 1990 census and the 1993 IPEDS surveys. Student enrollment data represent preliminary analysis of 1993 IPEDS figures. The list of the one hundred largest cities and metropolitan areas was obtained from 1990 census. (All these are currently being updated to reflect 2000 census and IPEDS figures.) Only institutions listed in *Accredited Postsecondary Education Institutions*, 1991 (Washington, D.C.: U.S. Department of Education, 1991) were included, and only institutions accredited by one of the six regional accrediting bodies were classified. Geographical placement was determined using addresses supplied by the colleges themselves. Colleges not clearly urban or suburban (according to ZIP code) were categorized as rural. Unit identification numbers assigned to each institution by IPEDS were used to run the classifications. The entire list of urban and suburban community colleges was examined to determine multicampus versus single-campus community college district. The names of each of these campuses were obtained through the *AACC Directory* (Washington, D.C.: American Association of Community Colleges, 1991) and the *Higher Education Directory* (Falls Church, Va.: Higher Education Publications, 1996). Where the campus name was not indicated, the college was asked to provide the official name used.

and public policymakers, particularly at the state level. Let us now turn our attention to specific descriptions of the categories.

Institutional Control. Writing more than four decades ago, as state appropriations were dramatically growing and new institutions were being created to serve the coming baby boom, John Corson (1960) noted that increased funding usually came with increased state regulation. The rise of the modern federal and state student financial aid system buttresses the rationale for a classification scheme that is inclusive of public as well as private nonprofit and proprietary two-year colleges. The nation's modern financial aid system dates to passage by Congress of the Higher Education Act of 1965, the Education Amendments of 1972, and the Middle Income Student Assistance Act of 1978, which created the modern Guaranteed Student Loan program. In the 2000 fiscal year, according to the Center for Policy Analysis of the American Council on Education (2001), some 9.4 million students received nearly $37.5 billion in federal guaranteed and direct student loans. State higher education agencies have much of the administrative responsibility for these loans.

Kerr's Carnegie Classification divided two-year colleges by type of institutional control—public and private—but did not make distinctions beyond that. The number of traditional private, nonprofit junior colleges, many of which were established prior to World War II, has dwindled to approximately 150 institutions. Nearly all of the two-year colleges established over the past fifteen years are for-profit colleges. In 1987, Carnegie documented 382 privately controlled two-year institutions; by 1994, that number had jumped to 508. The 2000 Carnegie Classification identified a total of 644 privately-controlled two-year colleges, an increase of 168 percent since 1987. In 2000, the Carnegie Classification disaggregated the private category, reporting 159 private nonprofit and 485 private for-profit associate's colleges (Carnegie Foundation for the Advancement of Teaching, 2001).

At a minimum, this indicates a dynamic marketplace within the private two-year sector. Some scholars have argued that federal and state student aid programs have worked to subsidize the establishment and expansion of proprietary institutions. They contend that proprietary expansion has often occurred at the expense of public universities and community colleges that, unlike private institutions, cannot discount their tuition. Alexander (2002) reports an increased percentage of total state appropriations, from 4 percent to 11 percent, funneled to private colleges through state direct grant aid programs, in the past decade.

We shall now turn to the use of geography, governance, and size in creating subcategories to further refine public community college classifications.

The Public Sector and Geographical Locale. The primary role states play in the direction, if not control, of publicly controlled community colleges is beyond dispute. Created under provisions of statutory enabling law and at least partly funded via annual or biennial legislative appropriations, public community colleges are legally recognized political subdivisions of the states that created them. Geographical service delivery areas for community colleges are typically defined by state statute or regulation through state coordinating boards, compelling evidence to use geography as a criterion in classifying public community colleges. Beyond the legal status lie practical issues implicit in the application of the Baldrige criteria described earlier: what works in a multicampus suburban or urban setting will not necessarily work in a rural setting.

The proposed classification scheme uses terms that describe the state-assigned geographical locale of the area served by the college—rural, suburban, and urban. If the physical address supplied by the colleges to the U.S. Department of Education for its IPEDS surveys lie within the one hundred largest metropolitan areas, the college is classified as either urban or suburban. In this classification scheme, any institution with a physical address outside the hundred largest standard or consolidated metropolitan statistical areas (SMSAs or CMSAs) is by definition rural. Colleges within the Census Bureau's definitions of SMSA or CMSA are either urban or suburban. If a multicampus suburban district has a rural campus but the physical address supplied by the college district is suburban, the community college is classified as suburban.

The matter gets a bit more complex in the nation's largest CSMA, the 21.2-million-person "New York–Northern New Jersey–Long Island, NY-NJ-CT-PA" CMSA. This CMSA contains both urban and suburban areas, including the central core areas of Newark and New York City. According to our classification scheme, Newark's Essex County Community College, with its Main and West Essex campuses, is a multicampus urban community college district, and Raritan Valley Community College is a suburban single-campus community college. Both institutions lie within the New York–Northern New Jersey–Long Island CMSA, yet the area is so large that it clearly constitutes more than one urban community college district. Our goal in defining urban colleges was to capture institutions that serve the urban core of America's central cities.

Initially, two methods of categorizing urban community colleges were contemplated: either obtaining a listing of America's hundred largest cities from the Census Bureau or using population density to determine urban areas from census figures. Although both were based on objective data, the former method was deemed preferable because states, not the Census Bureau, define community college delivery areas. Population density by itself does not bring meaning to community college classification. Our scheme uses objective data rather than self-reported institutional data to identify urban community colleges that are serving the inner-city cores of major metropolitan areas. Interestingly, in nearly every case, the central office of the urban multicampus district supplied to NCES/USED (the National Center for Education Statistics in the U.S. Department of Education) was in fact located downtown, a reality that buttresses this approach. It should be noted that making the urban-versus-suburban determination required not only the physical address of the institution but also access to metropolitan Census Bureau data, ZIP code directories, and in some cases actual maps.

The use of geography in classifying publicly controlled community colleges is also justified by historical precedent. When states set out to establish community college systems in the middle part of the twentieth century, a major policy justification was to extend access to *all* of the state's citizens. A close reading of the forty-nine state summaries included in the National State Community College Systems Information Project of the late 1980s and early 1990s confirms this point (Fountain and Tollefson, 1989; Tollefson, Garrett, and Ingram, 1999). The mission of extending access has not diminished as a result of the increased suburbanization of our nation's population in recent decades. Personal visits to over three hundred community colleges in thirty-four states and work at one of the nation's largest multicampus urban districts (Miami-Dade), as well as work with rural community colleges serving high-poverty regions of the nation, underscore this point.

It is my view that the very term "urbanicity" has a biased ring to it. The debate needs to be focused on equitable state policy: namely, providing universal higher education to all citizens. In this regard, rural is in no way *less* than suburban or urban, it is merely *different*. Use of the term *urbanicity*, from the IPEDS data set, is specifically rejected in favor of terms that more practically describe the state-assigned locale the institution serves.

To gain greater specificity, Tollefson and colleagues propose subcategories based on governance for the urban and suburban subcategories (multicampus and single-campus) and, for rural community colleges, large and small size. This classification scheme can help state policymakers acknowledge intrastate differences. In Ohio, for example, just six of the twenty-three independently governed community colleges receive revenue from local property taxes; four of the six are in suburban and urban areas. Illinois's challenge for three decades to adequately fund the community college campus in East Saint Louis is another example of the special role states have to ameliorate inequities. A classification scheme should assist policymakers in ensuring that students attending small community colleges in rural areas have access to the same array of general education and noncredit lifelong learning opportunities as students in suburban and urban areas do. Every study of which I am aware has documented a clear relationship between the geographical proximity of accessible institutions of higher education and increased college-going rates among the local populace.

Many authorities concerned with minority access have focused on increasing minority transfers from largely urban community colleges to achieve higher rates of baccalaureate degree success. Much of this work assumes that the baccalaureate degree is an automatic ticket to upward social mobility. Although many of the nation's urban community colleges are majority-minority, many community colleges in rural and suburban locales also have substantial minority student enrollments. Nationally, the enrollment of African Americans at small, rural community colleges described in Table 2.1 exceeds 10 percent. In the American South, it is not uncommon to find rural community colleges with African American enrollments in excess of 30 or 40 percent. Rural community colleges such as Frank Phillips College in the Texas Panhandle now have Hispanic student enrollments of 37 percent (fall 2001 enrollment, personal communication, Herbert J. Swender, April 16, 2002). The substantial dispersion of America's fast-growing Hispanic population documented in the 2000 census also argues for locale-neutral nomenclature.

Finally, the use of geographical locale is justified by the goal of community college comprehensiveness. This concept, as described by pre–Second World War community college scholars, assumed that general education and transfer as well as terminal (or vocational) programs to serve local needs would be offered. The goal was a broad curriculum that achieved better economies of scale. From the time of Leonard V. Koos (1924) and Walter Crosby Eells (1931), degrees for transfer were the associate in arts and associate in science, while other degrees, including the associate of applied science, nursing, business, and technology, were "terminal" (and therefore nontransferable). This bifurcation of functional mission was embedded in Kerr's classifications, which counted only the A.A. and A.S. degrees. Yet transfer occurs in ways not contemplated by early community college scholars such as Koos and Eells, and those multiple paths argue for inclusiveness of all types of associate degrees and indeed all types of two-year institutions. After all, practitioners, state policymakers, and scholars have long known that the vast majority of transferring students transfer without completing the associate degree, a point underscored by Cohen's longitudinal Transfer Assembly Project studies (Cohen and Brawer, 1996; Cohen, 1994) and also confirmed by NCES longitudinal studies of beginning students. Transfer has different meanings to students from different locales; for example, focus groups that I have conducted with students from colleges serving high-poverty rural areas have confirmed that for these students, the act of transfer meant physical separation from their home communities. Such physical relocation does not always occur in suburban and urban settings.

Public Rural Community Colleges and Size. In the rural public community college subcategory, small community colleges are those with enrollments below twenty-five hundred students; community colleges with higher enrollments are considered large. As the work of the Ford Foundation's Rural Community College Initiative and the American Association of Community Colleges' Rural Policy Roundtables reveals, small rural community colleges, with few exceptions, face special problems related to economies of scale and geographical isolation. It simply costs more to deliver high-quality services in a sparsely populated rural area, and the lack of economies of scale dramatically affects curriculum development and institutional planning. Concisely put, smaller size translates into higher costs (Katsinas, Opp, and Alexander, 2002). In contrast, large rural community colleges often have enrollments of forty-five hundred students and resemble their single-campus suburban counterparts in organizational complexity and function. The challenge of achieving economics of scale for small two- and four-year colleges was noted by the late Howard R. Bowen in *The Costs of Higher Education* (1980), which noted that state policy should take this issue into account. State policies in most places, however, do not. The challenge of economies of scale certainly applies as well to the tribally controlled colleges, most of which are located in remote rural areas.

If states wish to use their public community colleges to accomplish state policy objectives related to economic development and workforce training, it would do them well to recognize such geographical differences. Some states appear to be moving in this direction. In April 2002, for example, despite a very tight state funding picture for public higher education operating budgets, the Texas Higher Education Coordinating Board approved a proposal providing a budget base of $250,000 for the state's ten smallest rural community colleges as part of its budget proposals for the 2003 biennial session of the Texas legislature. Oklahoma has funding tiers for its small community colleges, and California has its Essential Community College funding provisions. According to my own research, fourteen states have some policy provision to allocate additional state funds to their rural community colleges. The role of state governments in providing funding equity for poorer K–12 school districts has been widely accepted by policymakers and the courts. State policymakers have a similar role for community colleges in order to promote equity in the delivery of programmatic access as well as economic development and workforce training.

Public Suburban and Urban Community Colleges and Governance. There is no question that the culture of a multicampus urban or suburban community college district differs greatly from that of a single-campus urban or suburban college. The sheer size and administrative complexity of a multicampus system that includes district functions such as marketing, academic affairs, financial aid, admissions, registration, business affairs, and institutional advancement requires a different skill set for district-level CEOs. This explains why advertisements for such positions typically cite the governance structure.

An important discovery made while analyzing the IPEDS data was that the federal government did not know precisely how many community colleges there are in the United States. The reason is that multicampus districts like the Maricopa Community Colleges in Phoenix, Arizona, reports data to IPEDS for its ten campuses *separately*, while Miami-Dade Community College in Florida reports data on its six campuses *as a single entry*. A more accurate tabulation of the total number of urban (and suburban) community college campuses creates a divisor that researchers and policymakers alike can use to disaggregate IPEDS and other data for better campus-to-campus and multicampus district comparisons.

Special-Use and Federally Chartered Institutions. In my classification journey, there were three initial categories of institutional control: public, private nonprofit, and proprietary. Later the factors of geography, governance, and size were used to develop more precise subcategories within the public sector. Unfortunately, this was still not exact enough to capture the diversity of two-year institutions.

The category of special-use institutions (SUIs) was created so that the scheme would be inclusive of all institutions awarding associate degrees. This specifically includes hospital-based allied health and nursing programs awarding associate degrees. Paul William Bober (1994) found four hundred radiologic technology programs in the United States, of which half were located at public community colleges and the other half at hospitals. A public hospital with associate degree allied health and nursing programs has the same state and federal financial aid policies and procedures with which to deal as public community colleges, if financially needy students are to be well served. The current shortage of allied health and nursing professionals underscores the state and federal policy interest in capturing all associate degree–granting institutions in a comprehensive classification scheme. Public hospitals should be included, but not in the public community college category. The SUI category also includes the Community College of the Air Force, which enrolls 373,000 registered students, and institutions that provide specialized training leading to associate degrees in such areas as funeral home management and embalming, theology, business, and paralegal studies (similar to the specialized institutions category for four-year institutions included in various editions of the Carnegie Classification).

Tribal colleges, which typically offer the associate degree as the highest degree awarded, also appear in the classification scheme. This is because state policymakers are increasingly thinking about creative ways to use tribal colleges to assist public policy goals. In a geographically large, sparsely populated state like Montana, single-parent majority students in the eastern Montana town of Wolf Point would probably rather attend the nearby tribal college, Fort Peck Community College, than to drive 162 miles to Dawson Community College, the nearest publicly controlled community college. Tribal colleges are not publicly controlled institutions. To capture the universe of two-year colleges awarding associate degrees, however, this scheme classifies them under the category "tribal colleges" in the more general institutional control category of "federally chartered and special-use institutions."

Conclusion

Early in my classification journey, I wrote to Clark Kerr and asked if Carnegie had ever considered classifying two-year institutions. It had not, he responded, adding that the task lay beyond the technical expertise of the Carnegie staff (personal communication, 1994). My long journey with classification makes me confident that the use of institutional control (public, private, and special-use) will inclusively capture the universe of *all* types of associate degree–granting institutions. In the public sector, choosing geography as a criterion is justified by the fact that alone among public higher education institutions, states *assign* the geographical service delivery areas to their community colleges. Finally, the use of governance (multicampus and single-campus) and size makes practical sense to distinguish institutions.

The very positive reaction to this nomenclature by practitioners participating in sessions at four different AACC conventions and at various presentations before community college audiences around the country over the years bolsters my confidence that these classifications do capture reality. They are not perfect, however; accepting "noise" is unavoidable in social science research. It is my hope that a meaningful, easy-to-use classification scheme will accomplish the same goal for the two-year college sector Kerr had in his original scheme: to improve the precision of research.

References

Alexander, K. F. "The Federal Government, Direct Financial Aid, and Community College Student." *Community College Journal of Research and Practice,* 2002, 26(7), 659–679.

American Council on Education Center for Policy Analysis. "Fact Sheet on Higher Education: Historical Trends in the Federal Guaranteed and Direct Student Loan Programs." [http://www.acenet.edu/resources/fact-sheets/historical-trends.pdf]. Retrieved September 6, 2001.

Bober, P. W. *Perceptions of Selection Criteria for Radiologic Technology Programs at Community Colleges.* Unpublished doctoral dissertation, Oklahoma State University, April 1994.

Bowen, H. R. *The Costs of Higher Education: How Much Do Colleges and Universities Spend per Student, and How Much Should They Spend?* San Francisco: Jossey-Bass, 1980.

Bowen, R. C., and Muller, G. H. (eds.). "Editor's Notes." In *Gateways to Democracy: Six Urban Community College Systems.* New Directions for Community Colleges, no. 107. San Francisco: Jossey-Bass, 1999.

Carnegie Foundation for the Advancement of Teaching. *The Carnegie Classification of Institutions of Higher Education, 2000 Edition.* Menlo Park, Calif.: Carnegie Foundation for the Advancement of Teaching, 2001.

Cohen, A. M. (ed.). *Relating Curriculum and Transfer.* New Directions for Community Colleges, no. 96. San Francisco: Jossey-Bass, 1994.

Cohen, A. M., and Brawer, F. B. *The American Community College.* (3rd ed.) San Francisco: Jossey-Bass, 1996.

Corson, J. J. *Governance of Colleges and Universities.* New York: McGraw-Hill, 1960.

Eells, W. C. *The Junior College.* Boston: Houghton Mifflin, 1931.

Fountain, B. E., and Tollefson, T. A. *Community Colleges in the United States: Forty-Nine State Systems.* Washington, D.C.: American Association of Community and Junior Colleges, 1989.

Katsinas, S. G. "Toward a Classification System for Community Colleges." Paper presented to the Council of Universities and Colleges, April 1993. (ED377925)

Katsinas. S. G. "Preparing Leaders for Diverse Institutional Settings." In J. C. Palmer and S. G. Katsinas (ed.), *Graduate and Continuing Education for Community College Leaders: What It Means Today.* New Directions for Community Colleges, no. 95. San Francisco: Jossey-Bass, 1996.

Katsinas, S. G., Opp, R. D., and Alexander, K. F. *Preserving Access with Excellence: Financing for Rural Community Colleges.* Chapel Hill, N.C.: MDC, 2002.

Koos, L. V. *The Junior College.* Research Publications of the University of Minnesota Education Series, no. 5. Minneapolis: University of Minnesota Press, 1924.

Tollefson, T. A., Garrett, R. L., and Ingram, W. G. *Fifty State Systems of Community Colleges: Mission, Governance, Funding, and Accountability.* Johnson City, Tenn.: Overmountain Press, 1999.

STEPHEN G. KATSINAS is the Don A. Buchholz Chair of Higher Education at the University of North Texas, where he directs the Bill J. Priest Center for Community College Education.

3

The author proposes and tests a community college classification based on curricular characteristics and their association with institutional characteristics. The analysis seeks readily available data correlates to represent the percentage of a college's course offerings that are in the liberal arts. A simple two-category classification system using total enrollment is ultimately found to be the most accurate.

A Curriculum-Based Classification System for Community Colleges

Gwyer Schuyler

The community college curriculum is an accurate representation of student course-taking behavior because it is comprised only of courses in which students enroll (courses are routinely canceled when minimum enrollments are not met). For the purposes of this project, the curriculum is understood as the complete set of courses that a college offers. In my doctoral dissertation, I propose a classification system for community colleges based on an institution's curriculum (Schuyler, 2000). A classification based on the curriculum would create meaningful categories. These categories would fit with people's impressions of an institution because the classification would be based on the actual courses offered by an institution. Students and staff at a particular institution know the extent of course offerings available; basing classification on course offerings will be in line with these experiences. This chapter is a brief overview of my dissertation research and proposal recommendations.

Methodology

This study is driven by the research question "How can colleges be classified based on curriculum characteristics?" Continuing in the tradition of earlier curriculum studies, the Center for the Study of Community Colleges (CSCC), under the direction of Arthur M. Cohen, has undertaken a periodic national survey of the community college curriculum. Beginning in 1975, the survey has involved the classification and counting of the number of course sections offered at a selection of public community colleges and the calculation of estimated student enrollments in certain academic areas. The data for this study are from the 1998 installment of the CSCC curriculum study.

To address the research question, the different dimensions on which to base the classification scheme will first be evaluated. Then the best classification scheme will be established by the use of descriptive and multivariate analyses—in particular, multiple regression analysis. Finally, the scheme will be applied to the colleges in the 1998 sample, and the results and implications of these findings will be discussed.

Sampling Methodology

Spring college catalogues and schedules were requested from approximately 950 public community colleges, and 459 usable sets were received. Colleges were listed in ascending order by enrollment and evenly divided into three size categories—small (2,748 students or fewer), medium (2,749 to 6,140 students), and large (6,141 students or more). To follow the sample size of a prior curriculum study, 164 sets of college catalogues and schedules were selected through stratified random sampling, based on a balanced distribution of colleges in the three size categories. The 164 college catalogues and schedules were reviewed and coded using a previously developed coding scheme adapted through the elimination of some coding areas and the addition of others. This coding scheme, which was originally developed in the 1970s by the Center for the Study of Community Colleges, was initially used solely for the exploration of the liberal arts curriculum, which included the disciplines of the humanities, social sciences, sciences, and mathematics. In later surveys, attention was given to the non–liberal arts curriculum, which was made up of vocational course offerings, and the coding categories were designed in collaboration with community college practitioners. Using this coding scheme, courses offered during the spring 2000 term were tallied and categorized and ultimately entered into an SPSS computer database. For the purposes of this study, each separate section of a course was counted (laboratory class sections, noncredit courses, and tutorials were excluded).

In the second phase of the study, requests for course enrollment data were sent to each of the 164 institutions. In total, 81 colleges submitted course-by-course enrollment printouts. Cross-referenced with the coded college schedules, enrollment figures from every fifth course on the enrollment printout were coded, tallied, and summed across the college sample to arrive at an estimated enrollment within each coding category. In addition, class sizes were extrapolated.

A Proposed Classification System

To construct a meaningful and practical categorization system for community colleges, institutional characteristics and their relationships to each other must be thoroughly analyzed. Characteristics of the curriculum and their relationships with other institutional characteristics are the focus of this proposed system.

An intuitive division exists between the colleges that focus on a liberal arts education (leading to transfer to baccalaureate-granting institutions) and those specializing in occupational training (leading to direct employment). Considering the variation in the percentage of liberal arts in the total curriculum, community colleges overall do differ greatly in their emphasis on liberal arts versus occupational education. My analysis will follow this intuitive distinction of liberal arts community colleges and occupational community colleges and further explore other institutional variables that relate to this curricular characteristic.

The Liberal Arts as the Basis for Classification

The percentage of liberal arts courses that a community college offers is a useful representation of the focus of the institution. From this one variable, one can interpret whether a college emphasizes the liberal arts or occupational training or if the college curriculum is equally balanced between the two.

A useful classification system is based on readily available information or data. If the characteristics on which a classification system is based are too difficult to come by, the process of classification no longer is feasible. The CSCC Curriculum Project compiled curricular data through a time-consuming process of collecting, analyzing, and coding college course schedules. This method is not practical unless it were to be adopted by the National Center of Education Statistics (NCES) in its standard data collection practices, which is not likely. Instead, the most practical and feasible approach would be to use existing data sets as the source of institutional data on which to base a classification scheme. By considering the relationships between curricular characteristics and other characteristics that are routinely measured by the NCES, a viable and meaningful classification model can be designed with readily available data acting as proxies for curricular characteristics.

Correlations among institutional characteristics reveal significant relationships between variables (see Table 3.1). Of special interest to this project are those variables that are correlated with the variable "percent liberal arts." Other curricular characteristics that are significantly positively correlated with this variable are "percent transfer" (percentage of courses offered that are transferable to a four-year institution), "percent remedial" (percentage of courses offered that were preparatory in nature and below college level), and "percent English." On the other hand, "percent business" is significantly negatively correlated with "percent liberal arts."

Looking at other institutional characteristics, "total enrollment" is significantly positively correlated with "percent liberal arts." In other words, institutions with higher numbers of students enrolled offer a greater percentage of liberal arts courses.

Table 3.1. Correlations Across Curricular Characteristics and Other Institutional Characteristics (N = 151)

Variable	*Percent Liberal Arts*
Percent transfer	.60**
Percent remedial	.33**
Percent English	.60**
Percent business	−.46**
Total enrollment	.32**
Total revenues	.26**
Total expenditures	.26**
Expenditures per student	−.30**
Percent total instruction expenditures	−.32**

**Significant at the .01 level.

With respect to details of expenditures and revenues, "percent liberal arts" is positively correlated with "total revenues" and "total expenditures." Thus colleges with larger revenues and expenditures have greater percentages of liberal arts offerings. This makes sense in light of the correlation between "total enrollment" and "percent liberal arts." Naturally, larger colleges have larger revenues and expenditures (as exemplified in the positive correlation of 0.88). This positive correlation reinforces the relationship between larger enrollments and larger percentages of liberal arts in the curriculum.

While "percent liberal arts" is positively correlated with "total revenues" and "total expenditures," it is negatively correlated with "expenditures per student." This means that those colleges that spend less per student have a greater percentage of liberal arts offerings and those that spend more per student have a greater percentage of occupational course offerings. A negative correlation is also found between "percent liberal arts" and "percent instruction expenditures." "Percent total instruction expenditures" represents the percentage of total expenditures that goes toward instructional costs such as faculty salaries and classroom supplies and equipment. This negative correlation is understandable in that there is less expense associated with classroom supplies and equipment in the teaching of the liberal arts than in the teaching of occupationally oriented courses.

Regression Analysis

Multiple regression analysis helps characterize the relationships of curricular and institutional characteristics. In this case, variables can be entered into a regression equation to see if they significantly contribute to the prediction of an institution's emphasis on liberal arts. Two stepwise multiple regressions were run, with "percent liberal arts" as the dependent variable in both. The first regression equation looks at curricular characteristics as predictors of the dependent variable. The second regression equation looks at financial characteristics as predictors of the dependent variable. In both cases, total enrollment is also included as an independent variable because of its significantly positive correlation with the dependent variable. To limit the scope of this analysis, a choice was made not to include "total instruction expenditures" as an independent variable even though it showed the same magnitude of correlation as "total enrollment."

The first regression was run to see the predictive power of other aspects of the curriculum, specifically, those aspects that are clearly definable and could be easily counted. Whereas tracking the variable "percent liberal arts" would require counting all courses offered by an institution to track variables such as "total English courses" or "total psychology courses," only a small fraction of the total course offerings of an institution need be counted. Keeping in mind the importance of clarity in the definition of the variable as well as the ease of quantifying the courses within the category, the following independent variables were selected:

- Total enrollment
- Curricular characteristics
    - Total English
    - Total psychology
    - Total biology
    - Total remedial
    - Total distance

Table 3.2 lists the variables that entered the first regression equation to predict "percent liberal arts" in the community college curriculum. Variables that entered the equation have a significance level of .05 or less.

The best predictor of percent liberal arts is the total number of English courses offered. Overall, English courses made up 22.8 percent of the total liberal arts curriculum in the sample of 164 colleges. This explains why the total number of English courses is the strongest predictor of the percentage of liberal arts courses in the curriculum—because English courses greatly contribute to that percentage.

The second variable to enter the regression equation is the number of distance courses. This variable is actually a negative predictor of percent liberal arts. This result can be understood in that many distance courses are

Table 3.2. Regression Predicting the Percent of Liberal Arts at Community Colleges

Independent Variable	*Simple R*	*Multiple R*	*Beta*
Total English	.36	.13	.36
Total distance	.41	.41	−.23

Note: Variables are shown in the order in which they entered the equation. (N = 164).

offered in the non–liberal arts field of business and office. Other than English courses offered and distance courses offered, the other independent variables did not enter the regression equation.

For the second multiple regression, institutional characteristics associated with revenues and expenditures were included. The following institutional characteristics were selected as independent variables:

- Total enrollment
- Expenditure characteristics
  - Expenditures per student
  - Percent instruction expenditures
  - Percent scholarship expenditures
  - Percent faculty salary expenditures
- Revenue characteristics
  - Percent state appropriations
  - Percent federal appropriations
  - Percent local appropriations
  - Percent auxiliary revenue

Table 3.3 lists the variables that entered the regression equation to predict percent liberal arts in the community college curriculum.

From the results of this regression, the most predictive institutional characteristic of percent liberal arts in the curriculum is the total enrollment of the institution. The more students enrolled at an institution, the greater the percentage of liberal arts courses in the curriculum. The other three variables that entered the regression equation entered as negative predictors. The percentage of expenditures that go toward instructional costs is a negative predictor of the percentage of liberal arts courses, meaning that the greater the percentage of expenditures that go toward instructional costs, the less the percentage of liberal arts courses in the curriculum. In other words, colleges typically spend more per student in occupational programs. Similarly, the percentage of revenues from auxiliary services is also a negative predictor of percent liberal arts, meaning that the greater the percentage of revenues that comes from auxiliary services of the institution, the less the percentage of liberal arts in the curriculum. Finally, the amount that a

Table 3.3. Regression Predicting Percent of Liberal Arts at Community Colleges

Independent Variable	*Simple R*	*Multiple R*	*Beta*
Total enrollment	.34	.12	0.34
Percent instruction expenditure	.46	.21	−.30
Percent auxiliary revenue	.49	.24	−.18
Expenditures per student	.52	.27	−.19

Note: Variables are shown in the order in which they entered the equation ($N = 151$).

college spends per enrolled student is a negative predictor of the percentage of the curriculum devoted to the liberal arts.

From these two regression analyses, it can be concluded that both curricular characteristics and other institutional characteristics can be used as predictors of the extent that the curriculum is focused on the liberal arts. In terms of curricular characteristics, the total number of English courses is the best predictor of the percentage of liberal arts in the curriculum.

In terms of financial characteristics, the predictive power of the expenditure and revenue characteristics is not as strong as that of total enrollment of the institution. First and foremost, total enrollment is a positive predictor of the percentage of liberal arts in the curriculum. After considering college size, a more refined prediction of the percentage of liberal arts in the curriculum can be made by considering the percentage of expenditures going toward instruction, the percentage of revenue coming from auxiliary functions, and an institution's expenditures per student.

Proposed Categories

The categories described here have been constructed to classify community colleges. Although a classification system can include any number of categories, I have, in order for categories to be intuitive as well as accurate and for the classification process to remain simple, limited the number of categories to two:

Occupational community colleges: Less than 50 percent of the total curriculum is in the liberal arts.
Liberal arts community colleges: 50 percent or more of the total curriculum is in the liberal arts.

So that the classification system remains practical, proxies must be used to sort colleges into these two categories. Based on the regression analysis, two approaches are proposed—one based on curricular characteristics and one based on institutional financial characteristics.

Total Enrollment as a Proxy

Because of the statistically significant positive correlation between a college's total enrollment and the percentage of liberal arts courses it offers, the characteristic of total enrollment may be a good proxy for categorizing colleges based on their emphasis on the liberal arts. Although it is not as powerful a predictor as the curricular characteristic of the number of English courses or distance courses offered, it did enter the regression equation before any revenue or expenditure variables.

Total enrollment would be a convenient variable on which to base classification because it is readily available through the NCES. However, it is too simplistic to imagine that an accurate classification system could be designed using total enrollment alone. Instead, total enrollment may be most useful when used in conjunction with other characteristics that correlate with and predict the percentage of liberal arts in the curriculum.

Expenditures as a Proxy

Percent expenditures on instructional costs can act as a negative proxy of the liberal arts emphasis of the curriculum. This approach would not require any extra data collection since the expenditure information is already collected by the NCES. From these data, colleges can subsequently be sorted into the proposed two categories. Based on the total student enrollment, colleges that have greater than average percentage expenditures on instruction for the size of the institution would be classified as occupational. Those that have less than average percentage expenditures on instruction for the size of the institution would be classified as liberal arts.

English Courses as a Proxy

The number of English courses associated with the total courses offered and total student enrollment would be another way to sort colleges into the two categories. Based on the total student enrollment, colleges that have a lower than average number of English courses for the size of the institution would be classified as occupational. Those that have a greater than average number of English courses for the size of the institution would be classified as liberal arts.

This approach would require some data collection through the counting of English course offerings and total number of course offerings. However, these data could be added to the information that institutions currently report to the NCES.

Testing the Proposed Classification System

Of the total sample of 164 colleges, 108, or 66 percent, have a curriculum that is made up of a majority of the liberal arts; 34 percent have a curriculum that is majority occupational.

Having established the actual classification of the colleges based on the percentage of liberal arts in the curriculum, the next step is to explore and test the proxy models.

Testing of Proxy Classification Models

For the models that considered college size, colleges were divided into categories based on total student enrollment. The enrollment categories were as before: small, 2,748 students or fewer; medium, 2,749 to 6,140 students;

and large, 6,141 students or more. The mean values of the criterion variables were calculated in each size category or for the sample as a whole. A college was classified on the basis of where the values of its criterion variables fell—either below or above the mean or within a specified percentage of it. The accuracy of each model—and more specifically, of each cell in each model—was determined by comparing each college's classification in that model to the actual classification based on the percentage of courses actually offered in the liberal arts. The percentage of accurate classifications was subsequently computed.

The model that was found to represent the most accurate classification system possible derived from the tested variables is shown in Table 3.4.

The practicality of this classification system may be limited at present because it would require that all community colleges report both the total number of English courses offered and the total number of courses overall. Yet this analysis has shown that the percentage of English courses offered is the best predictor of the extent that a college emphasizes the liberal arts. If the National Center for Education Statistics were to add this to the reporting schedules, more meaningful and more descriptive categories of community colleges could be devised. Unfortunately, the chances that such new data would be collected are slim. Hence the best-fitting system that uses data that are already collected for all institutions would be a simple categorization based on size alone.

Table 3.5 shows that large colleges were classified correctly as liberal arts colleges in 93 percent of the cases. Small to medium colleges, by contrast, were accurately classified as occupational colleges in only 52 percent of the cases. Consequently, if this system were to be followed, it would be more accurate to have only two categories: small to medium colleges (with a range of curricular emphases) and large liberal arts colleges. The first category would include colleges that are both occupational and liberal arts (see Table 3.6). Because no accurate proxy has been identified to sort the small to medium colleges, the category should remain undivided.

Table 3.4. Classification Model: Three Categories of Size by Two Categories of the English Proxy

Category	*Criterion: English Courses in Relation to Mean for Colleges of This Size*	*Percentage of Colleges Accurately Classified*
Occupational		
Small	<mean	79
Medium	<mean	67
Large	<mean	14
Liberal arts		
Small	>mean	75
Medium	>mean	84
Large	>mean	100

Table 3.5. Combined Small and Medium Categories and Large Category by Two Categories of Curricular Content

Category	*Criterion: Size*	*Percentage of Colleges Accurately Classified*
Occupational	Small to medium	52
Liberal arts	Large	93

Table 3.6. Most Accurate Classification System Tested: Using College Size Alone

Category	*Percentage of Colleges Accurately Classified*
Small to medium colleges	100
Large liberal arts colleges	93

Importance of Classification

Classification, however rudimentary, is useful as a starting point. The project of revising the classification of community colleges would not have been proposed if a current classification of the system of higher education did not already exist. Thus classification schemes stretch one's cognitive understanding of the classified objects, allowing perspectives that might not otherwise have been explored.

Second, classifications can always be improved and refined. In fact, the failure to fit objects within a classification system fuels revision. Emerging from this research, one area for further consideration would be the use of total instructional expenditures in a community college classification system, since this variable showed a high negative correlation with the offering of liberal arts courses.

It is my sincere hope that the proposed categories of community colleges will further the refinement of the Carnegie Classification of Institutions of Higher Education. Let it be one step in a long process of improvement.

Reference

Schuyler, G. L. "A Curriculum-Based Classification System for Community Colleges." Unpublished dissertation, University of California, Los Angeles, 2000. (ED451884)

GWYER SCHUYLER holds a Ph.D. in higher education and organizational change from the University of California, Los Angeles. She is an academic counselor at Santa Barbara City College.

4

College size is a valid, readily available, easily understood, and nonjudgmental criterion that relates directly to other important college characteristics. Therefore, size should be considered the main criterion in the classification of community colleges.

College Size as the Major Discriminator

Arthur M. Cohen

Classifying community colleges is similar to classifying other sectors of higher education only in that, like university leaders, community college spokespersons look carefully to see where their institution is ranked and complain if its position doesn't match their belief about where it ought to be placed. This behavior is understandable because college leaders live in a world of public relations and tend to categorize all reports about their institutions as either laudatory or inimical. If a report praises college accomplishment, it is valid; if it casts any aspect of the college in a bad light, it is invalid. And if it provides a reliable analysis, it is disaggregated to determine which parts are valid or invalid according to the criteria noted. Furthermore, they contend, their institutions have multiple missions, and so any attempt to collapse categories or aggregate data inevitably minimizes some things they consider important. College leaders also find it difficult to recognize that regardless of their institution's uniqueness, classifications must be based on available data, collected systematically across institutions.

But the overriding reason why many community college leaders have resisted classification systems is their experience with reports based on incomplete or erroneous information. Several researchers have reviewed data showing that students entering community colleges are less likely to receive bachelor's degrees and concluded that the institutions contribute to maintaining the American social class structure by diverting students

The author wishes to thank Rozana Carducci, Kim Peterson, and Victor Saenz for their help in collecting data for this chapter.

from their dreams, conveniently ignoring the fact that for most beginning students the choice is not between the community college and the freshman class at a university but between the community college and no participation in higher education. Analysts sometimes erect faulty premises, such as "Although the vast majority of community college students transferred to four-year institutions up until the late 1960s. . . . , in recent years the percentage of students who transfer has declined significantly" (Shaw and London, 2001, p. 92). In fact, there has never been a time when a majority of community college students transferred to universities, but in their eagerness to disparage the role of the contemporary community college, the analysts create a golden era that never existed (Dougherty, 1994).

Even worse, many researchers draw inappropriate conclusions from flawed data. Persistently, they ask beginning students, "What is the highest academic degree that you intend to obtain?" (Sax, Astin, Korn, and Mahoney, 2001), "What is the highest level of education you ever expect to complete?" (National Center for Education Statistics, 1998), or, wondrous to relate, "If there were no obstacles, what is the highest academic degree you would like to attain in your lifetime?" (Hagedorn and Maxwell, 2002). Between 40 and 60 percent of the respondents choose master's, M.D., Ph.D., or other advanced degree. These data are meaningless since few eighteen-year-olds have made objective plans for advanced study or entertain the notion that their opportunities will ever be curtailed. However, some researchers, blind to the absurdity of the question they have asked, incorrectly conclude that the community college has depressed students' educational attainment. Other college-based researchers seeking information on students' aspirations ask the more valid question "What is the main reason you are enrolled in this college at this time?" and obtain answers useful in demonstrating college contribution to student progress.

Criteria

Taking cognizance of the state of research on community colleges and the ways that college leaders react to it suggests that the first criterion for any classification system is that the resulting information must be descriptive but not hierarchical. The colleges must not be grouped in a way that permits commentators to question why a particular college is not doing better on one or another variable. College leaders understandably loathe questions such as "Why aren't you in line with the state average on degrees awarded (or jobs gained or students transferring)?" Such queries usually yield headlines claiming "Latest Data Show Local College Falling Short."

Second, the criteria must be valid. Using such measures as "research funds received" or "size of endowment" is useless; too few community colleges have a visible presence in these areas. Nor is it useful to compute "degrees awarded as a percentage of enrollment." This comes closer to the community college purpose, but it assumes that all enrollees are degree seekers and omits an estimate of the value gained by students who transfer short of receiving a degree or who gain employment short of program completion. Furthermore, a sizable percentage of students enroll in short-term programs for the purposes of job upgrading or skill development; many already have academic degrees. A measure using an outcome as a percentage of something demands a valid denominator.

Third, the data used in a classification scheme must be readily available. It is futile to create categories for which special surveys must be done in order to find data to put into them. All colleges have data on many aspects of their students, faculty, curriculum, and other areas, but these data are not collected uniformly across institutions. Most state agencies collect data uniformly for the colleges in their jurisdiction, but definitions vary across state lines. The most reliable national data come from the National Center for Education Statistics' Integrated Postsecondary Education Data System (IPEDS). And the data required by IPEDS include such categories as total enrollment by sex, attendance status, race or ethnicity, age, and disability status; full-time and part-time faculty and staff characteristics and salary; degrees awarded; student charges; and institutional wealth, income, and expenditures (National Center for Education Statistics, 2001). Unless IPEDS expands its categories, those who would classify community colleges are fairly well limited to those data.

Last, the categories must be readily understandable. There's not much point in creating a complex formula in which institutions are classified by computing such arcana as "ratio of part-time students to class size as related to college location, age of faculty, and value of physical plant." Applying high-powered statistical tests to these relationships adds nothing useful. The categories must be discrete as well as meaningful.

Categories and Relationships

Within the limits that must be placed on any classification system, it is possible to classify community colleges according to valid, readily available, easily understood, nonjudgmental criteria. The main criterion should be college size. Numerous studies dating back over several decades show that college size is correlated with several important variables. Schuyler concluded, "The most predictive institutional characteristic of the percent liberal arts in the curriculum is the total enrollment of the institution" (2000, p. 77). And Phipps, Shedd, and Merisotis reported that "size of institutional enrollment is the most distinguishing characteristic of public 2-year institutions" (2001, p. iv).

The relationships between size and such variables as percentages of full-time and part-time students and faculty, percentage of revenue received from federal grants and contracts and from auxiliary sources, and per capita expenditure on instruction were tested using IPEDS data, which were available for sixty-nine of the eighty colleges in the sample of colleges provided for this analysis. The variable "total students" yielded colleges with enrollments ranging from 476 to 20,799 students. Splitting the sixty-nine colleges equally into high, medium, and low categories allowed the placement of twenty-three colleges in the high group (6,282 students or more), the medium group (2,740 to 6,281 students), and the low group (2,739 students or fewer) on each of the variables.

College size proved related to four other factors:

- *Percentage of college income derived from federal government grants and contracts (FGGC).* Ten of the twenty-three largest colleges were among those receiving the highest amount of FGGC as a percentage of their total income. Reciprocally, twelve of the colleges with the lowest percentage of FGGC were among the smallest colleges.
- *Expenditures on instruction as a percentage of total education and general expenditure (TEGE).* Ten of the colleges with the highest ratio of expenditure on instruction were among the smallest colleges, whereas only four of the high instruction-cost colleges were in the large-size category.
- *Percentage of part-time students.* Nine of the colleges with the highest percentages of part-time students were large; thirteen of the colleges with the lowest percentage of part-time students were small.
- *Percentage of auxiliary revenue.* Ten of the colleges with the highest percentage of total current fund revenue accounted for by auxiliary revenue were among the largest colleges.

The percentage of full-time faculty also showed some distinctions:

- *Percentage of full-time faculty.* Half the colleges with the lowest (32 percent or less) ratio of full-time faculty had the lowest (33 percent or less) percentage of full-time students.
- *Federal government grants and contracts.* Nine of the colleges highest in full-time faculty were also in the upper third of the group in terms of the percentage of their income from FGGC.

Although data on curriculum are not readily available, that criterion is so important that curriculum counts were made for each of the sampled colleges for which IPEDS data were also retrieved. Class schedules for the spring or fall term in 2002 were collected from the colleges, and class sections were counted and coded according to liberal arts or non–liberal arts emphasis. Overall, 55 percent of the sections were liberal arts and 45 percent non–liberal arts, a finding almost exactly matching the 54–46 tabulations made in the Center for the Study of Community Colleges' 1998 national survey (Schuyler, 2000) and the 56–44 breakdown in the 1991 national survey (Cohen and Ignash, 1994).

The curriculum counts were tabulated separately for the colleges with the largest and the smallest enrollments. The largest third of the colleges in the sample presented 57 percent of their classes in the liberal arts, 43 percent in trade, business, technical, and avocational (physical education, personal interest) areas. In the smallest third, 44 percent of the classes were liberal arts, 56 percent in non–liberal arts fields. (Not surprisingly, many of the small colleges highest in non–liberal arts areas had the word *technical* in their name.)

Discussion

The observed relationships yield a pattern of colleges differentiated by clusters of variables, with size as the most distinctive among them.

As related to curriculum, the bigger the institution, the higher the percentage of students enrolled in English, humanities, science, social science, and mathematics—the traditional liberal arts. This finding is readily explainable. Imagine a college with five thousand students enrolled, and suppose that a duplicated head count shows five thousand students taking classes in the liberal arts and two thousand in technical education, personal skills, health fields, and trade and industry courses. Double the size of that college, and enrollment in the liberal arts courses doubles while they move hardly at all in the occupational areas. Why? Because enrollments in occupational curricula tend to increase only as new programs are added. A program in nursing that enrolls 150 students is likely to enroll 150 students regardless of the overall college enrollment; the same goes for programs in engineering technology, auto mechanics, or protective services. Furthermore, a high proportion of students plan on transferring, and bachelor's degree requirements in universities are weighted toward the liberal arts. Some flagship universities, including those in Texas, Illinois, and California, offer few undergraduate occupational majors, and where they do, liberal arts courses are required nonetheless. Overall, the universities usually expect transferring students to have completed a sizable proportion of their general education requirements at the community college.

The smaller colleges spend more on instruction per FTE (full-time equivalent) student, first, because their curriculum is weighted toward the non–liberal arts and colleges tend to spend more per student in occupational programs. The health service fields demand clinical settings and laboratory space. Computer and engineering technologies demand equipment, as do the programs training mechanics. Indeed, the reimbursement schedules in many states reflect this differentiation. Illinois colleges receive 14 percent more per capita for students in technical programs and 43 percent more for those in health fields (Illinois Community College Board, 2001). A second reason is that because nearly all the expenditure on instruction is attributable to faculty salaries, and the cost of an instructor in a classroom is unrelated to college size, the economies of scale appear in the relatively lower cost of administration and physical plant operation in the larger institutions. Thus instruction commands a higher percentage of educational and general expenditures in the smaller colleges.

The larger colleges received greater proportions of their income from federal government grants and contracts and from auxiliary revenue sources. They are probably more able to afford grant proposal writers, alumni development staff, and other entrepreneurs to find opportunities for income-producing ventures.

Size related also to student attendance patterns, with the larger colleges higher in percentage of part-time enrollments. Those colleges have a greater variety of programs, tend to be located in urban areas where outside employment opportunities are more prevalent, and are likely to be in proximity to other higher education institutions where concurrent enrollment patterns are feasible.

The relationship of FGGC to percentage of full-time faculty suggests that the instructors with greater involvement with their institution and their discipline are also involved in seeking extramural support. The almost exact match between percentage of full-time faculty and full-time students reflects the national numbers, where 60 percent of the faculty and 65 percent of the students are part-timers. As numerous studies of faculty have shown, the full-timers relate quite differently to their work.

Conclusion

Using college size as a criterion yields some interesting patterns showing how community colleges differ. Visualize two colleges. One is in the large size category and has a low percentage of per capita expenditures on instruction and a high percentage of auxiliary revenue and of part-time students. A second college is smaller but is high in percentage of per capita expenditures on instruction and low in percentage of part-time students and in revenue from other than traditional sources. What inferences can we draw? We can predict that the first college is likely to be high in liberal arts curriculum with a high student transfer rate and low in business and industry collaborations. The second college probably awards more occupational certificates and has a lower percentage of liberal arts course offerings.

Is the second college better or worse than the first? No one can say. It merely has a different emphasis, and that's what a classification system seeks to reveal. The criteria have served as proxies for many other college characteristics.

Any number of other classifications may be entertained as long as they are valid, based on readily available, easily understandable, and nonserial data. They should also bear a verifiable relationship to other important criteria. The categories outlined in this chapter offer a good starting place because they relate to variables that community college analysts consider to be the institutions' main missions: prebaccalaureate study, occupational education, and community service and collaborations. And size is the variable that relates most directly to other important college characteristics. The large colleges tend to have the highest percentage of income from FGGC and from auxiliary revenue and the highest percentage of part-time students. The small colleges have lower percentages of part-time students and a higher ratio of expenditure on instruction.

If IPEDS were to expand its data collection categories, information on students' course-taking behavior could be useful. Separate studies done under Office of Educational Research and Improvement auspices have related students' course completion with such data as degrees earned, length of time to degree, and dropout and persistence. They have also pointed up how students switch majors and the magnitude of remedial studies (Adelman, 1992). Since a major purpose of the entire higher education enterprise is enhancing student learning as evidenced by course completion and degree awards, detailed data on these phenomena collected routinely and consistently would be useful.

Less useful for purposes of classifying community colleges but interesting for understanding institutional contributions might be an annual tally of the percentages of the eighteen- to forty-four-year-old population in a college's service area that enrolls. A match of statewide enrollment figures with census data showed that figure varying from under 2 percent in Alaska, Indiana, and Louisiana to 8 percent or more in Washington and Wyoming (Cohen and Brawer, 2003, pp. 57–58). Since the community colleges draw well over 90 percent of their students from within commuting distance, data on the percentage of the local population that attends could be revealing.

Many state agencies collect data on college outcomes and processes: student retention, percentage of population attending college, licensure exam pass rates, and transfer rates, to name a few. But until such data are produced uniformly nationwide, they cannot be reliably employed in a college classification system. Still, the IPEDS data show that the nation's community colleges are not amorphous or homogeneous. Each has unique characteristics that have been shaped by its history and by the ways in which it has responded to its constituents. Using valid data to categorize the colleges in a nonnormative way can only aid in understanding them.

References

Adelman, C. *The Way We Are: The Community College as American Thermometer.* Washington, D.C.: U.S. Department of Education, 1992. (ED338269)

Cohen, A. M., and Brawer, F. B. *The American Community College.* (4th ed.) San Francisco: Jossey-Bass, 2003.

Cohen, A. M., and Ignash, J. M. "An Overview of the Total Credit Curriculum." In A. M. Cohen (ed.), *Relating Curriculum and Transfer.* New Directions for Community Colleges, no. 86. San Francisco: Jossey-Bass, 1994.

Dougherty, K. J. *The Contradictory College.* Albany: State University of New York Press, 1994. (ED369461)

Hagedorn, L. S., and Maxwell, B. *Research on Urban Community College Transfer and Retention: The Los Angeles TRUCCS Project.* Los Angeles: Rossier School of Education, University of Southern California, 2002. (ED464662)

Illinois Community College Board. *Operating Budget Appropriation and Supporting Technical Data for the Illinois Public Community College System, Fiscal Year 2002.* Springfield: Illinois Community College Board, 2001.

National Center for Education Statistics. *Descriptive Summary of 1995–96 Beginning Postsecondary Students.* Washington, D.C.: U.S. Department of Education, 1998. (ED425684)

Phipps, R. A., Shedd, J. M., and Merisotis, J. P. *A Classification System for 2-Year Postsecondary Institutions.* Washington, D.C.: National Center for Education Statistics, U.S. Department of Education, 2001. (ED453896)

Sax, L. J., Astin, A. W., Korn, W. S., and Mahoney, K. M. *The American Freshman: National Norms for Fall 2001.* Los Angeles: Higher Education Research Institute, Graduate School of Education and Information Studies, University of California, Los Angeles, 2001.

Schuyler, G. L. "A Curriculum-Based Classification System for Community Colleges." Unpublished dissertation, University of California, Los Angeles, 2000. (ED451884)

Shaw, K. M., and London, H. B. "Culture and Ideology in Keeping Transfer Commitment: Three Community Colleges." *Review of Higher Education,* 2001, 25, 91–114.

U.S. Department of Education. *Integrated Postsecondary Data System.* Finance survey (for public institutions), fiscal year 1999. Washington, D.C.: U.S. Department of Education. Retrieved April 16, 2001, from [http://www.nces.ed.gov/iped/form1999/f-1.pdf].

ARTHUR M. COHEN is director of the ERIC Clearinghouse for Community Colleges and professor of higher education at the University of California, Los Angeles.

5

This chapter explores the development of a classification system for two-year institutions that can provide a framework for analysis and contribute to the discourse in public policy. The proposed classification system is based on cluster analyses using data from the National Center for Education Statistics' Integrated Postsecondary Education Data System (IPEDS).

Using IPEDS to Develop a Classification System for Two-Year Postsecondary Institutions

Jamie P. Merisotis, Jessica M. Shedd

One of the most important and most enduring ways in which classification systems are used is for governmental, system, and institutional policy development. Classification systems are involved in allocating funds, comparing institutional inputs and outputs, and making decisions about faculty, students, and staff. At the national level, establishing a meaningful classification system for two-year institutions that is supportive of and necessary to policy development and research is limited by the extent to which appropriate data for the universe of two-year institutions are collected.

In attempting to construct a national system of classification for two-year institutions, the sources of data are regrettably limited. The most comprehensive of these data sources is the Integrated Postsecondary Education Data System (IPEDS). IPEDS is the core postsecondary education data collection program in the U.S. Department of Education's National Center for Education Statistics (NCES). It encompasses *all* institutions and educational organizations whose primary purpose is to provide postsecondary education. Data are collected from more than ten thousand postsecondary accredited and nonaccredited institutions, including baccalaureate and higher degree granting institutions, two-year award institutions, and less-than-two-year institutions. The IPEDS system is built around a series of interrelated surveys that collect institution-level data on enrollment, program completion, faculty, staff, finances, and academic libraries.

In conducting the analysis for this chapter, we have chosen to take an explicitly empirical approach to classification of two-year institutions through the use of the IPEDS data sets. Such an approach allows the classification system to be replicated by others and to be modified over time to take into account the changing nature of individual institutions. This makes this type of classification system ideal for policy purposes, since policy decisions must take changing circumstances into account.

IPEDS defines a two-year institution as a school with at least one program of at least two years' but less than four years' duration leading to the school's highest degree or award. This chapter draws from the 1997–98 Institutional Characteristics IPEDS Survey of Federal Title IV participating two-year institutions, as well as from previous analyses conducted for the National Center for Education Statistics (2001).

Title IV participation was chosen as the central criterion for inclusion for several reasons, including the importance of federal Title IV student financial aid in federal policy development, the basic determination of quality that goes into the Title IV institutional eligibility process, and the importance that states and others tie to Title IV requirements. It is important to emphasize that this universe includes private for-profit institutions, because these "proprietary" institutions are often excluded from research on two-year institutions. In total, 2,068 of the 2,427 two-year institutions with Title IV participation agreements are included in the analysis.

Data Limitations

Due to limitations in the IPEDS data with respect to information on two-year institutions, there are several aspects of these institutions that could not be examined. IPEDS surveys collect more data from degree-granting institutions than from two-year institutions that offer only certificates. For example, the age of enrolled students and many financial data elements are collected only from degree-granting institutions. This restricted the analysis that could be performed on non-degree-granting institutions.

Aspects of two-year institutions that could help distinguish these schools from one another are not collected on the national level. Lists of programs offered are not available, and noncredit coursework is not captured, even though noncredit activity is often a large part of the curriculum and student enrollment at many two-year institutions. In addition, some institutions are part of a multicampus system while others are single-campus institutions—a status that is difficult to determine from IPEDS data because institutional governance is not included as a variable in the data set.

Methodology

There are many possible methods of analysis to arrive at a classification scheme; we have chosen to use a combination of *k*-means cluster analysis and descriptive statistics. Cluster analysis is the generic name for a variety of procedures that can be used to create a classification. These multivariate statistical procedures attempt to arrive at mathematically formed "clusters" or groups of relatively homogeneous entities based on measures of similarity or difference with respect to specific variables. (For a detailed discussion of cluster analysis procedures, see Aldenderfer and Blashfield, 1984.)

The choice of variables to be included in the *k*-means cluster analysis is one of the most critical steps in the process and probably has "the greatest influence on the ultimate results of a cluster analysis" (Anderberg, 1973, p.12). Because the analysis uses an aggregate mean, each variable that is included in the analysis affects the clustering results. Ideally, variables should be chosen within the context of a theory used to support the classification and serve as the basis for the choice of variables to be used. It is also possible that during the cluster analysis process, certain clusters may be so "natural and self-evident as to. . . . be revealed by almost any method" (p.23). If certain variables or clusters present themselves as obvious candidates for categorization, it is appropriate to remove either the variable or the group of cases and continue the analysis with the remaining subset or subsets of data.

For our purposes, cluster analysis was supplemented with various procedures in order to find the "best" variables and categorization. These procedures are described next.

Literature Review and Focus Group Meeting. A review of past research addressing the classification of two-year institutions provided the initial direction for considering variables for cluster analysis. To add to this, a focus group of seven experts familiar with two-year institutions was convened. The focus group provided a starting point for the analysis by offering feedback on potential variables for classification based on their availability, usefulness for public policy purposes, and relevance to the two-year postsecondary education community.

Preliminary Analysis. Twenty potential variables were selected by the focus group. The variables that were available through IPEDS were then further examined, based on their range and variance and their replicability. Each variable had to show a wide range and variance among the institutions so that there was the potential to create distinguishable categories. In addition, the variables and classification system as a whole had to be replicable so that the classification system designed would continue to be useful in the future and could be refined and updated when necessary.

The Chosen Variables. The variables that remained either after the preliminary analysis on the universe of institutions or the preliminary analyses that were later conducted on each sector of two-year institutions relate to enrollment, student demographics, and institutional characteristics that include awards granted and financial characteristics. Exhibit 5.1 provides a comprehensive list of the variables and their definitions.

Cluster Analysis with Two-Year Institutions. Correlated variables were determined from both correlation matrices and hierarchical cluster analyses of the variables themselves. Highly correlated variables such as

Exhibit 5.1. Definitions of Variables That Remained After Preliminary Analyses and Were Included in Cluster Analyses

Variable	*Definition*
Urbanicity or location	Degree of urbanization of the institution's location.[a] 1. Large city 2. Mid-size city 3. Urban fringe of large city 4. Urban fringe of mid-size city 5. Large town 6. Small town 7. Rural
Twelve-month unduplicated head count	Unduplicated head count of undergraduates enrolled during the twelve-month period.
Percentage of full-time, first-time degree-seeking students	Full-time, first-time degree-seeking undergraduate enrollment (twelve-month unduplicated head count) as a percentage of total undergraduate enrollment (twelve-month unduplicated head count).
Percentage of part-time students	Part-time undergraduate enrollment (fall enrollment) as a percentage of the total fall enrollment.
Percentage of minority students	Minority student enrollment (fall enrollment) as a percentage of the total fall enrollment. "Minority" includes students who are black, Hispanic, non-Hispanic, American Indian or Alaskan Native, and Asian or Pacific Islander.
Percentage of non-traditional-aged students	Nontraditional-aged student enrollment (fall enrollment) as a percentage of total fall enrollment. "Non-traditional-aged" includes students age twenty-five and older. These data are collected only for degree-granting institutions.
Percentage of part-time faculty	Part-time faculty as a percentage of total faculty on staff.
Percentage of awards granted as certificates	Number of certificates granted as a percentage of total awards granted.
Percentage of awards granted in allied health programs	Awards, certificates, and degrees granted in allied health programs as a percentage of the total awards granted. "Allied health programs" include all programs identified in the NCES's Classification of Instructional Programs (CIP) as "Health Professions and Related Sciences."
Percentage of awards granted in occupationally specific programs	Awards, certificates, and degrees granted in occupationally specific programs as a percentage of total number of awards granted. "Occupationally specific programs" include all programs identified in the NCES's CIP as "instructional programs whose expressed intent is to impart work-related knowledge and skills at the secondary and postsecondary levels."
Percentage of education and general (E&G) expenditures for instruction	Expenditures on instruction as a percentage of the total current fund E&G expenditures.

Exhibit 5.1. (Continued) Definitions of Variables That Remained After Preliminary Analyses and Were Included in Cluster Analyses

Variable	*Definition*
Percentage of E&G expenditures for scholarships and fellowships	Expenditures on scholarships and fellowships as a percentage of the total current fund E&G expenditures.
Percentage of revenues from state and local support	Revenue from state and local appropriations, grants, and contracts as a percentage of the total current fund revenue.
Institutional control	Control of the institution—public, private not-for profit, or private for-profit.

Source: National Center for Education Statistics, Integrated Postsecondary Education Data System (IPEDS), 1997 Full Collection Year.

[a]For more information, see National Center for Education Statistics, 2001.

institutional enrollment and the percentage of part-time students enrolled were run in separate cluster analyses in order to avoid overstating their value in the analysis.

Postanalysis. Once the cluster analysis was completed, "driver" variables—those variables that statistically demonstrated the highest ability to differentiate among institutions—were considered both on their own and in combination with other variables through the use of scatterplots, cross-tabulations, and frequency distributions. The variables that created the most distinct categories were chosen to guide the classification system.

The Classification System

The following narrative describes the classification system for two-year institutions and outlines the rationale underpinning its development. A description of the categories of two-year institutions is provided along with the characteristics of each.

Institutional Control of Two-Year Institutions. The results of the analysis across the universe of two-year institutions showed that institutional control is a distinguishing characteristic of these schools. The cluster analysis pointed toward three highly correlated variables: percentage of revenues from state and local appropriations, grants, and contracts; institutional enrollment; and percentage of students enrolled part-time. All three of these variables are highly correlated with institutional control, strongly indicating that they were serving as proxies for control. This was also compelling given that institutional control is typically accepted as a reasonable means for grouping institutions and organizing classification models. The three categories are public institutions (N = 1,029), private not-for-profit institutions (N = 309), and private for-profit institutions (N = 730).

In the remainder of this chapter, generalizations are made about the institutions that fall into each category. These generalizations are derived from two sources: the descriptive statistics of variables from the IPEDS data and a review of the actual institutions in each category. It is important to note that these generalizations may not be true for all institutions in that category but are intended to clarify how the categories differ.

Public Institutions. Public institutions have a higher median enrollment (4,318 students) than the other two sectors of institutions in addition to having a higher median percentage of part-time students (58 percent). These institutions have a lower median percentage of full-time, first-time degree-seeking students enrolled (12 percent) and a lower median percentage of awards granted that are certificates (30 percent)—the lowest of all the sectors. Institutions in the public category also have a higher median percentage of part-time faculty or staff (61 percent) than both categories of private institutions and, not surprisingly, have a much higher median percentage of current fund revenues from state and local support (56 percent). Public two-year institutions are more likely to be located around an urban area (median = 3, urban fringe of a large city).

Private Not-for-Profit Institutions. Private not-for-profit institutions have the smallest median enrollment of the three sectors (138 students) and a low median percentage of part-time students (4 percent), and they tend to be located in more urban locations (median = 2, mid-size city). This group of institutions has a median of 100 percent for the percentage of awards granted that are certificates, the percentage of awards granted that are in occupationally specific programs, and the percentage of awards granted in allied health fields.

Private For-Profit Institutions. Like the private not-for-profit institutions, the private for-profit group of institutions tend to be located in more urban locations (median = 2, mid-size city). These institutions fall in the middle of the three sectors with respect to median enrollment (254 students) but have the lowest median percentage of part-time students (0 percent). On the other hand, they tend to have a high median percentage of full-time, first-time degree-seeking students enrolled (63 percent)—the highest of the three sectors. Like the not-for-profits, these institutions have a median of 100 percent awards granted in occupationally specific programs, and they have a high median percentage of awards granted that are certificates (96 percent). However, of the three sectors, the for-profit institutions have an extremely low median percentage of awards granted in allied health programs (0 percent) and a relatively low percentage of educational and general (E&G) expenditures for instruction (27 percent).

The Remaining Analysis

All further analyses were conducted separately on each of the subgroups described. Each variable was examined again, based on *range and variance*, to determine if it was appropriate for the particular subgroup of institutions that was being investigated. Correlated variables in each subgroup were

Figure 5.1. Classification System of Two-Year Institutions

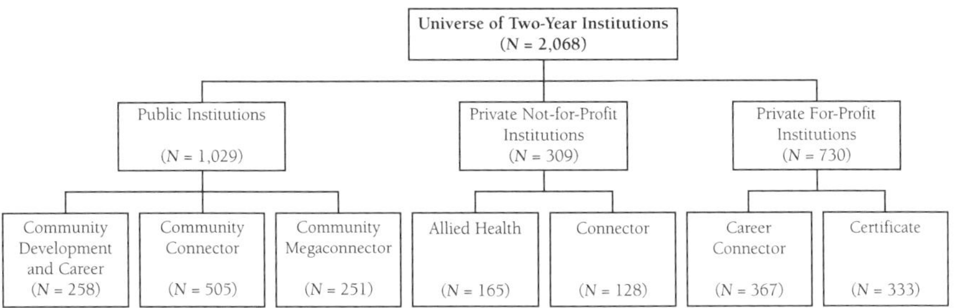

Note: The sum of the number of institutions in each category does not add to the total number of institutions due to missing data in the variables chosen for categorization. In the universe of 2,068 institutions analyzed in this report, 61 institutions could not be placed in a final category: 15 public 2-year institutions, 16 private not-for-profit institutions, and 30 private for-profit institutions.

Source: U.S. Department of Education, National Center for Education Statistics, Integrated Postsecondary Education Data System (IPEDS), 1997 Full Collection Year.

identified and run in separate cluster analyses to avoid skewing the results. The resulting classification system consists of the following: three categories for public institutions, two categories for private not-for-profit institutions, and two categories for private for-profit institutions, as illustrated in Figure 5.1.

Once the categories were determined, they were named by examining the characteristics of the institutions in each category. When naming the categories that were formed, an emphasis was placed on creating names that were not value-laden. One of the goals was to design a classification system for two-year colleges that was nonhierarchical so that one category would not be seen as more desirable than another. As noted earlier, the names for all seven categories were developed by analysis of the IPEDS variables and a review of the actual institutions in the category.

The terms *connector* and *community* are used in the names of several categories across institutional control. *Connector* indicates that the institution provides a connection between two- and four-year institutions by facilitating articulation. *Community* suggests that the institution emphasizes meeting the workforce needs and demands of the community in which it is located. It is important to note, however, that the names of the categories created are meant as broadly descriptive terms. They are intended to describe most of the institutions that fall into the given category but are not necessarily precisely accurate in each specific case.

Public Two-Year Institutions

Institutional enrollment is the most distinguishing characteristic of public two-year institutions and is clearly the driving variable for differentiating one public institution from another. The cluster analysis, in conjunction with postanalyses, indicated that institutional enrollment on its own is the best at creating categories with different characteristics; other variables did not appear to add to the differentiation of these institutions. After examining many different options for separating the institutions by enrollment, using the 25th and 75th percentiles seemed a reasonable option, as it clearly created categories that differed from one another. For ease of analysis and policy discussion, these percentiles were rounded to 1,999 students (less than 2,000 students) and 9,999 students (less than 10,000 students). Three distinguishable categories were created for public two-year institutions: community development and career institutions, community connector institutions, and community megaconnector institutions.

The three categories of public institutions are displayed in a radar graph to better illustrate the differences and similarities among them (see Figure 5.2). The median values of eight variables characterizing the categories are plotted on axes scaled from 0 to 100 percent. The shape of the plot for each category can be quite informative. For example, in Figure 5.2, the shape of the plots for the community connector and community megaconnector categories are similar, indicating that the categories have similar characteristics with only a few exceptions. It is also quite noticeable that the community development and career institutions grant a much higher percentage of their awards in occupationally specific fields and also tend to grant a high percentage of their awards as certificates. (Similar radar graphs for the private not-for-profit and the private for-profit categories will be presented later in this discussion.)

Figure 5.2. Characteristics of the Categories for Public, Two-Year Institutions, According to Selected Variables (Median Values are Plotted)

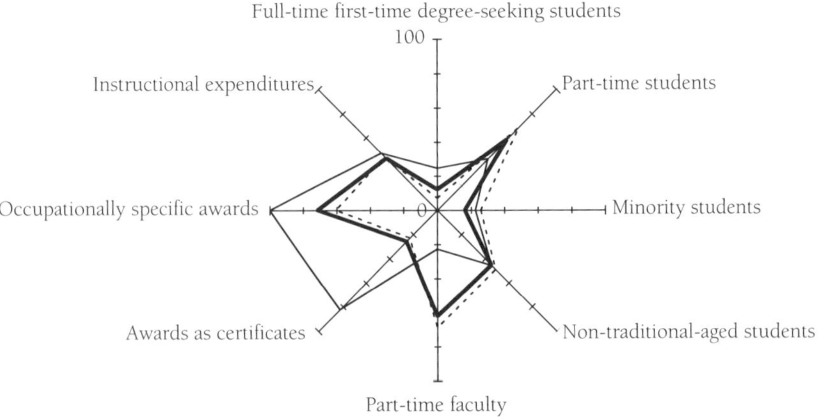

Community Development and Career Institutions. This category includes institutions with fewer than 2,000 students enrolled. These institutions tend to be in less urban locations than the larger community connector and community megaconnector institutions—the median location for institutions in this category is a small town (median = 6, small town). Community development and career institutions have a lower median percentage of part-time students enrolled (42 percent) and a higher median percentage of full-time, first-time degree-seeking students enrolled (25 percent) than the other categories of public institutions. There is a tendency for a higher percentage of awards granted at these institutions to be certificates (median = 82 percent) and a higher percentage of awards granted in occupationally specific programs (median = 100 percent) than at institutions in the other two categories. Finally, community development and career institutions have a smaller median percentage of part-time faculty (23 percent) than the community connector and community megaconnector institutions do.

More interpretively, community development and career institutions tend to be schools that confer awards and degrees primarily in job and career skills development for students and to focus on overall workforce development for the communities they serve. Most of these schools are located in rural areas, which are often not served by proprietary schools. Therefore, these institutions frequently offer certificate programs usually found in private for-profit schools that tend to be located in more urban areas.

Community Connector Institutions. This category consists of schools with enrollments of 2,000 to 9,999 students. With 505 institutions, this is the largest category in the classification system. These institutions are generally not found in as urban locations as the community megaconnector institutions but tend to be in more urban locations than the community development and career institutions. Community connectors fall in the middle of the three categories for median percentage of part-time students (59 percent) and for median percentage of full-time, first-time degree-seeking students (12 percent). A lower median percentage of minority students is enrolled (16 percent) at these institutions compared to both other categories of public institutions. Compared to the community development and career institutions, these schools have a low median percentage of their awards granted as certificates (26 percent)—similar to the median percentage of the community megaconnectors. These institutions fall in the middle of the three categories for median percentage of their awards granted in occupationally specific programs (71 percent). Finally, community connectors have a higher median percentage of part-time faculty (62 percent) on staff than the community development and career institutions.

When looking at the institutions in this category, it appears that they tend to confer awards and degrees that target job and career skills development and to offer academic programs with some general education that can facilitate transfer to four-year institutions. These institutions tend to enroll a large number of part-time students and often have a high percentage of part-time faculty on staff. In addition, they offer a wide variety of programs and may be important feeder schools for colleges and universities in the surrounding area. Remedial education may also be an important function of these institutions.

Community Megaconnector Institutions. Institutions in this group each have at least 10,000 students enrolled. They tend to be in more urban locations than institutions in the other categories of public institutions (median = 2, mid-size city). These institutions have the highest median percentage of part-time students enrolled (69 percent) and the lowest median percentage of full-time, first-time degree-seeking students enrolled (7 percent) of the public institution categories. Community megaconnector institutions grant a similar median percentage of their awards as certificates (23 percent) as the community connector institutions but a lower median percentage when compared to the community development and career institutions. Community megaconnectors also grant a lower median percentage of their awards in occupationally specific programs (60 percent) compared to the other two groups of public institutions. Finally, this group of institutions tends to have the highest median percentage of part-time faculty (69 percent)—though it is only slightly higher when compared to the community connector institutions.

A further look at community megaconnectors and the data we have described implies that these schools are predominantly urban institutions that tend to confer awards and degrees that target job and career skills development and to offer academic programs with some general education that can facilitate transfer to four-year institutions. These institutions, which often offer a wide array of programs, resemble four-year universities more than many of the other community colleges. According to research by Schuyler (2000) that identified a relationship between enrollment and curriculum, these larger institutions tend to offer more liberal arts courses. Of the awards they grant, a relatively higher percentage are degrees and are in programs that are not occupationally specific. However, it is important to note that a high percentage of the full-time, first-time student body is non-degree-seeking. These institutions are often known for providing educational services at night or on the weekend and often enroll high percentages of part-time students and students over the age of twenty-four. Finally, these large institutions, most often found in urban areas, frequently have more than one campus in the city.

Private Not-for-Profit Two-Year Institutions

The percentage of total awards granted that are in allied health programs is the distinguishing characteristic of private not-for-profit two-year institutions. Based on the frequency distributions, cross-tabulations with other

Figure 5.3. Characteristics of the Categories for Private, Not-For-Profit Two-Year Institutions, According to Selected Variables (Median Values are Plotted)

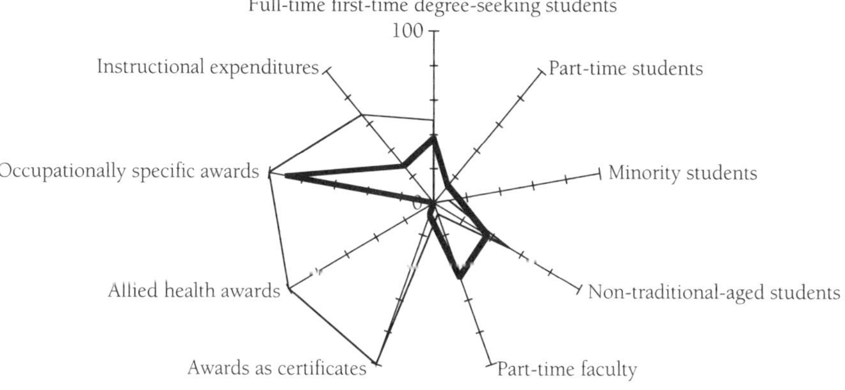

variables, and scatterplots, the percentage of total awards granted in allied health programs stood out as an obvious way for the private not-for-profit institutions to be differentiated. Analysis of the descriptive statistics of the characteristics of the categories indicated that further categorization of this group of institutions was not necessary. Using this variable, two distinguishable categories of private not-for-profit institutions were formed and then named to reflect their characteristics as derived from both the IPEDS data and a review of the actual institutions in the category. The final categories for this sector are allied health institutions and connector institutions (see Figure 5.3).

Allied Health Institutions. By definition, allied health institutions grant 100 percent of their awards in allied health programs. These institutions tend to be located in urban areas (median = 2, mid-size city). Compared to connector institutions—the other category of private not-for-profit institutions—allied health institutions tend to have much smaller enrollments (median = 69), a much lower median percentage of part-time students enrolled (0 percent), and a lower median percentage of minority students enrolled (9 percent). On the other hand, allied health institutions have a higher median percentage of full-time, first-time degree-seeking students enrolled (50 percent) and a higher median percentage of non-traditional-aged students enrolled (52 percent). Because allied health programs are, by definition, occupationally specific programs, 100 percent of awards granted by allied health institutions are in occupationally specific programs. In addition, these institutions have a high median percentage of awards that are granted as certificates (100 percent). Finally, allied health institutions have a much lower median percentage of part-time faculty (7 percent) and a much higher median percentage of E&G expenditures for instruction (67 percent).

Connector Institutions. This category consists of private not-for-profit institutions that do not grant 100 percent of their awards in allied health programs. These institutions tend to be located in urban areas (median = 2, mid-size city). The institutions in this category also tend to have larger enrollments (median = 436), a higher median percentage of part-time students (13 percent), and a lower median percentage of full-time, first-time degree-seeking students (38 percent) than allied health institutions. Connector institutions have a lower median percentage of non-traditional-aged students (37 percent) but a higher median percentage of minority students enrolled (15 percent) than allied health institutions. These institutions have a low median percentage of certificates awarded (8 percent), and although the percentage of awards granted in occupationally specific programs is less than that of the allied health institutions, connector institutions still tend to confer a high percentage of their awards in occupationally specific fields (median = 89 percent). Finally, these institutions have a higher median percentage of part-time faculty (46 percent) but a much lower median percentage of E&G expenditures for instruction (28 percent).

From the data presented and from examining the institutions in this category, the connector institutions seem to be larger than the allied health institutions; however, the former are still small in enrollment size. Connector institutions are schools that tend to confer awards and degrees that target job and career skills development and to offer some academic programs with some general education that can facilitate transfer to four-year institutions for those students who wish to continue their education. This category consists of a mix of institutions, many of which confer all of their awards in occupationally specific programs. Depending on their interests, users of this classification system may consider further dividing this small group of institutions by the percentage of awards granted in occupationally specific programs.

Private For-Profit Two-Year Institutions

Virtually all institutions in this sector are found in urban locations and grant a high percentage of their awards in occupationally specific programs. These variables were not included in this particular subanalysis because they are nearly universal and do not discriminate. The percentage of total awards granted that are certificates is a distinguishing characteristic of private for-profit two-year institutions. Based on cluster analysis and subsequent analyses on the driving variables within this institutional sector, the percentage

Figure 5.4. Characteristics of the Categories for Private, For-Profit Two-Year Institutions, According to Selected Variables (Median Values are Plotted)

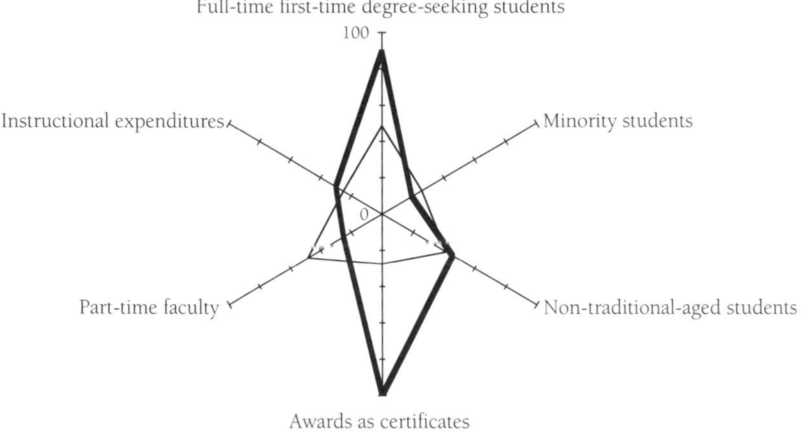

□ Career connector (367 institutions, median enrollment 391)
■ Certificate (333 institutions, median enrollment 102)

of total awards granted that are certificates creates two distinguishable categories that were then named to reflect IPEDS data and a review of actual institutions in the respective categories: career connector institutions and certificate institutions (see Figure 5.4).

Career Connector Institutions. This category consists of institutions that grant less than 100 percent of their awards as certificates—at least one of their awards conferred is in the form of an associate degree. The median percentage of awards granted as certificates is 28 percent. The median enrollment at institutions in this category is 391 students—higher than the median enrollment for certificate institutions. Career connector institutions have a lower median of full-time, first-time degree-seeking students (51 percent) but a higher median percentage of part-time faculty on staff (48 percent) than certificate institutions do. The median location for institutions in this category is a mid-size city (median = 2).

The private for-profit career connector institutions are degree-granting institutions—although many also offer certificates—that target job and career skills development for students. Many of these institutions offer academic programs with some general education that can facilitate transfer to four-year institutions for those students who wish to continue their education. Located almost exclusively in urban areas, these relatively small schools concentrate their program offerings in occupations that are in high demand, particularly technology and business. A larger percentage of their students are minority (26 percent).

Certificate Institutions. These institutions grant 100 percent of their awards as certificates, as opposed to associate degrees. The institutions in this category tend to be located in more urban locations—they are most often found in a mid-size city (median = 2). As a group, they tend to have smaller enrollments than career connector institutions—the median enrollment is 102 students. Certificate institutions have a high median percentage of full-time, first-time degree-seeking students (77 percent) when compared to the career connector institutions. Finally, these institutions have a rather low median percentage of part-time faculty (25 percent).

Certificate institutions tend to give specialized training, usually in a single job category or area, preparing students to proceed directly into the workforce. The vast majority are located in urban areas and enroll many full-time students with the goal of obtaining a certificate or award. This category includes a high concentration of schools focusing on cosmetology services. Many of the programs offered at these institutions require state certification.

Conclusion

The impetus behind the development of a new classification system for two-year institutions is that the present systems—all with their own strengths—do not fully and adequately describe this vital sector of the postsecondary community. The criteria considered essential for this analysis are the following:

- *The data must be collected at the national level.* Our data source was the National Center for Education Statistics' Integrated Postsecondary Education System (IPEDS). This comprehensive system collects data on enrollment, program completion, faculty, staff, finances, and academic libraries from all postsecondary institutions.
- *Each variable, and the classification system as a whole, must be replicable.* This ensures that the classification system will continue to be useful in the future. Since the variables used in the classification system are all derived from IPEDS, they are available to anyone who wishes to analyze them. Furthermore, the variables used are collected on a consistent basis.
- *The classification system must have a manageable number of categories, and each institution should reside in only one category.* Our classification scheme resulted in seven mutually exclusive categories: three categories in the public sector, two in the private not-for-profit sector, and two in the private for-profit sector.
- *The classification system must make policy-relevant distinctions among institutions.* The variables chosen from the IPEDS data collection system are useful with regard to policy development and institutional research. Some examples of these variables include student enrollment; percentage of full-time, first-time degree-seeking undergraduates; percentage of part-time

students; and percentage of minority students. However, it cannot be overlooked that many policy-relevant data elements central to the mission of two-year institutions are not collected at the national level. For example, information on the specific curricular offerings of institutions would be quite useful. This limitation notwithstanding, several variables did relate to the functions of two-year institutions and were therefore relevant to research and policy analysis.

- *The categories must be descriptive and not evaluative or hierarchical.* The variables employed to categorize institutions are those that are commonly used and value-neutral. Care was taken to choose category names that did not suggest a hierarchy so that institutions within a particular category will not feel pressured to "move up" to another category because of a perceived higher ranking.

Although community colleges and other two-year institutions often share many qualities, such as a commitment to open access and responsiveness to local needs, they are in fact a disparate group of institutions. The goal in creating this classification system for two-year institutions is to provide a new framework for policy discussions and a basis for research and analysis.

References

Aldenderfer, M. S., and Blashfield, R. K. *Cluster Analysis.* Thousand Oaks, Calif.: Sage, 1984.

Anderberg, M. R. *Cluster Analysis for Applications.* Orlando, Fla.: Academic Press, 1973.

National Center for Education Statistics. *A Classification System for 2-Year Postsecondary Institutions.* Washington, D.C.: U.S. Department of Education, 2001.

Schuyler, G. L. "A Curriculum-Based Classification System for Community Colleges." Unpublished dissertation, University of California, Los Angeles, 2000. (ED451884)

JAMIE P. MERISOTIS is president of The Institute for Higher Education Policy in Washington, D.C.

JESSICA M. SHEDD is a former research analyst at The Institute for Higher Education Policy and is currently a research analyst in the Office of Institutional Research and Planning at the University of Maryland.

6

Community colleges are often thought to constitute a separate sphere in higher education, one that is unique and largely self-contained. This chapter calls into question that basic assumption, demonstrating that the price an individual community college charges is a function of the role and place that the institution occupies in the overall market for postsecondary education. The analysis suggests a classification that distinguishes colleges with respect to their emphasis on formal degree programs versus delivery of courses.

On Markets and Other Matters: A Price Model for Public Two-Year Colleges

Susan M. Shaman, Robert Zemsky

For American higher education, taxonomies are a tough sell. Fundamentally, colleges and universities argue that what they do defies simple classification. No one wants to believe that one's institution can be pigeonholed—clustered together with a mass of other institutions like peas in the same pod.

Still, the fascination with type and taxonomy remains, spurred at least in part by the one classification system that has dominated American higher education for the past three decades. The Carnegie Classification of Institutions of Higher Education began with the assumption that institutions could in fact choose what they wanted to be—a liberal arts college, a research university, a comprehensive institution, or for that matter, a community college. The terms in the classification had meaning, not as part of a derived taxonomy but as standards that institutions could elect to pursue. Thus liberal arts colleges knew that they were at risk of losing their "liberal arts" designation if they offered too much "professional" training or allowed their master's programs to become more than modest appendages. Comprehensive and doctoral institutions, on the other hand, knew exactly what they had to do in order to become research universities: prior to 2000, awarding fifty doctorates each year and receiving $15.5 million annually in sponsored research support.

These classifications, shaped by Clark Kerr during his tenure as head of the Carnegie Commission on Higher Education, shared many of the same assumptions that Kerr had embedded in the California Master Plan he brought to fruition in the 1960s. Those assumptions focused primarily on how institutional planning and enlightened public policy could help shape institutional futures. And both levers worked, as long as an institution's mission was the product of coherent and conscious design. By the mid-1980s, however, it was clear that something quite different was beginning to shape institutional futures. Markets and market forces—and the competitive spirals they engendered—were making a mess of the top-down categories that had so successfully guided the master plan and the Carnegie Classification. Institutions both public and private were discovering that their financial future increasingly depended on their ability to attract students, on the one hand, and to charge market-based prices, on the other. To do both, an institution had to offer what the market wanted and only afterward ask whether the institution's new programs were a good fit with its historic mission.

A Market Taxonomy

Once markets came to matter, the obvious question became "Is there an alternative way of classifying or at least pegging institutions so that the structural nature of the higher education market becomes more apparent?" The technical answer to that question was yes—precisely because markets are systems in which price both matters and is predictable. Put another way, if markets had indeed come to shape higher education, then it ought to be possible to develop a model and accompanying classification system using market characteristics or markers to predict the prices institutions charge.

We had earlier developed and refined a market taxonomy for four-year degree-granting institutions that explained a substantial proportion of the variance in the prices these institutions charged per year of undergraduate education (Zemsky, Shaman, and Shapiro, 2001). This market or pricing model identified a limited number of market segments that when linked to the Carnegie Classification helped explain which institutions were likely to employ large numbers of part-time faculty, which would prove attractive to particular ethnic groups, and which would likely pay higher salaries to their faculty. Not so coincidentally, it turned out that the price models could also predict which institutions *U.S. News and World Report* would list at the top of its rankings.

The prices that this four-year model proved least successful at predicting were those charged by institutions that served the "user-friendly" or "convenience" segment of the market: institutions that enrolled substantial numbers of part-time students, who often pursued their baccalaureate education one course at a time and at a variety of institutions. Given that finding and the general assumption that community colleges make up a separate sphere within higher education, we guessed that our market segment model would miss the most important elements of a community college market—if in fact there was a community college market as opposed to a community college sphere. Yet we were intrigued by the invitation to extend our analysis and classification of postsecondary markets to include community colleges. So we accepted the challenge, assuming that truly substantial changes in the basic model would have to be made to reflect the unique and predominantly local role that community colleges had come to play in the American system of higher education.

In Pursuit of a Market Model for Two-Year Colleges

We could not have been more wrong! Both the general modeling strategy we had developed for segmenting the four-year higher education market and most of the resulting model's specifics could be readily applied to the market in which community colleges compete—demonstrating in the process that community colleges are in fact subject to the same market pressures as institutions that grant baccalaureate degrees. The analysis depended on the completion of three linked tasks: identifying a set of two-year institutions for which sufficient data were available, identifying a dependent variable that adequately captured the prices community colleges charged, and identifying a set of independent or predictor variables that might be capable of explaining the prices two-year institutions charge.

Identifying a Set of Two-Year Institutions. The best available data source for two-year institutions proved to be the federal government's Integrated Postsecondary Educational Data System (IPEDS) and its array of detailed information reported by nearly every college and university in the United States. Although both private and public two-year colleges report their data to IPEDS, most of the market variables our model required were not consistently available for the private institutions in the set. Accordingly, the base data set includes only the 644 public two-year institutions for which recent (1999–2001) IPEDS data contained valid values for most of the variables thought to be important to the model's construction. In the end, the taxonomy was applied to a further reduced set of 566 institutions for which IPEDS provided the requisite enrollment and degree data.

Defining a Dependent Variable Capturing the Prices Community Colleges Charge. The process for defining the model's dependent variable began with an initial approximation of the price definition used in the models for four-year colleges and universities. In that analysis, the price a given institution charged was calculated by the sum of its revenues from tuition, fees, and public appropriation minus institution-supplied financial aid, divided by full-time-equivalent (FTE) enrollment. Despite its predictive power in the price model for the four-year sector, this definition of a *calculated price* simply did not work for two-year colleges; we could not build a credible model using a definition of price that incorporated the subsidy provided through public appropriation. What did work, however, was a simpler definition in which a *net price* was calculated for each institution by taking tuition and fee revenue minus institutional financial aid expenditures and then dividing that sum by that institution's FTE enrollment.

Selecting Independent Variables. The list of candidate independent variables was drawn from the basic enrollment, program, and financial data institutions reported to the federal government through IPEDS. Given that our price model used regression analysis to predict the *net price* that public two-year institutions charge their students, our analytic goal was to identify the limited number of independent variables that both substantially reduced the variance in the dependent or price variable and also made intuitive sense to practitioners and policymakers (see Exhibit 6.1).

Degree Production. The process of identifying a best set of independent variables began with a focus on degree production mirroring the four-year model's use of completion rates to segment the market for baccalaureate education. Some two-year institutions actively serve a credentialing market, as evidenced by the large proportion of their students who actively pursue associate degrees, certificates, or diplomas. Other two-year colleges serve individuals who either are not seeking a credential or are treating their education as an incremental process that can occur over a substantial number of years. Still other two-year institutions serve two masters: a cadre of students who are credential-seekers and another set who are principally course-takers.

This first independent variable focusing on degree production was defined as the ratio of degrees to enrollments—that is, the proportion of

Exhibit 6.1. Price Model Variables for Two-Year Institutions

Variable	*Definition*
Net price per FTE student (dependent variable)	Total tuition and fee revenue minus institutional financial aid expenditures, divided by FTE enrollment (FTE defined as full-time plus one-half of part-time)
Degree production ratio	Degrees awarded divided by total enrollment
Cohort graduation rate	Reported percentage of initial cohort of certificate and associate's degree-seekers (as defined by the institution) who graduated in 150 percent of expected time
Local appropriations as a percentage of total government appropriations	Local government funding as a percentage of all government funding
Government appropriations as a percentage of core revenue	All government funding as a percentage of total revenue minus auxiliary revenue
Underrepresented minorities as a percentage of total enrollment	African American, Hispanic, and Native American students as a percentage of total enrollment
Region	Any of six regions of the United States (middle states as the reference category)
Urban setting	Location in a large or mid-size city (based on U.S. Census Bureau definition of a metropolitan statistical area)

Source: National Center for Education Statistics, Integrated Postsecondary Education Data System (IPEDS), 1999 and 2000 Collection Years.

an institution's students who were awarded a degree in any given academic year.

Degree Attainment. To complement this variable, a second one focusing on degree attainment was added to reflect the experience of institutions that have within the student body a well-identified cohort who are seeking associate degrees or certificates and for whom well-defined programs are designed and implemented. To capture this dimension of two-year collegiate programs, IPEDS now asks each institution to report the proportion of an initial cohort of entering students that earn their credentials in 150 percent of the normal completion time. Hence for a typical associate degree that may be completed in two years, the variable examines what proportion of an initial cohort achieves its goal within three years. The actual specification of the cohort is left up to the institution. One of the ironies, then, is that although we never know exactly how a given institution defined a cohort, the designation itself plays a significant role in predicting the price the institution charges.

Interaction Effect Between Degree Production and Cohort Graduation. At any given institution, the cohort graduation rate may or may not be related to the degree production ratio. An institution not primarily concerned with degree programs may nevertheless serve a small cohort of students who are pursuing a degree or certificate. To the extent that this subset of students is successful at completing the degree, the institution will show a high cohort graduation rate while producing a relatively low degree production ratio. Still, for most institutions, there is a moderately strong correlation between the two variables. For this reason, an interaction effect was calculated and became part of the final price model to express the combined impact of degree production and cohort graduation rates.

Interaction Effect Between Proportion of Government and Local Support. Although public appropriations for community colleges could not be treated as a price discount (as in the pricing model for four-year institutions), such subsidies play a substantial role in shaping the pricing of individual two-year institutions. To account for the role played by public financing, two variables were included in the model. The first was the proportion of each institution's operating budget derived from government funds. The second was the proportion of that support obtained from the local community, provided primarily through local taxes. This latter variable captures an earlier finding that the source of funding—state versus local—plays a significant role in structuring key educational inputs as well as outcomes in the community college (National Center for Postsecondary Improvement, 1998). Again, the final price model included a variable capturing the interaction between the two variables.

Student Demographics. To determine whether demographic characteristics of the student body—ethnicity, gender, and age—might play a role in explaining net price, data on these elements were examined. The availability of data on student age was sporadic at best, and gender did not play a significant role in the model. Ethnicity, on the other hand, proved to be a significant variable and was included in the final price model.

Institutional Setting. Finally, variables defining institutional setting for two-year colleges—including both the urban or nonurban character of the campus and the region of the country in which it is located—were included in the final price model. While regions capture something about the economies of different parts of the country, we hesitated to introduce state-level analysis because that would require adding too many variables to this preliminary model.

A Market After All

The final model, presented in Table 6.1, is, frankly, not what we expected. This model is robust, is intuitively satisfying, and accounts for a considerable fraction—nearly two-thirds—of the variance in net price per FTE student. At the same time, the fact that the model identifies the degree production ratio and the cohort graduation rate as significant predictors of price tells us that the pricing model for two-year institutions tracks surprisingly well with the four-year price model. Indeed, one of the central aspects of the model is the combined role of the degree production ratio and the cohort graduation rate. The more degrees (including certificates) per enrolled student an institution produces, the higher its predicted net price per FTE student, all other things being equal. The higher an institution's cohort graduation rate, the lower its predicted net price per FTE student, all other things being equal. The interaction of these two variables indicates that institutions with high cohort graduation rates, remembering that only a portion of the students are included in the denominator of this calculation, are often the same institutions with low degree production ratios—when all students are included in the denominator. The magnitude of the impact of increases in either of these two variables depends on the value of the other. At successively higher values of the cohort graduation rate, the impact of an increase in the degree production ratio is amplified. At increasingly higher values of the degree production ratio, the negative effect of an increase in the cohort graduation rate is reduced.

Consider some illustrations of this relationship for institutions close to the median value and 75th percentile on these two measures. When the cohort graduation rate is 20 percent, the net price per FTE student is predicted to increase by $26.30 for every 1 percent increase in the degree production ratio. If the cohort graduation rate is 30 percent, then the net price per FTE student is predicted to increase by $32.95 for every 1 percent increase in the degree production ratio.

At the same time, if the degree production ratio assumes a value of 10 percent, then the net price per FTE student is predicted to drop by $18.81 for every 1 percent increase in the cohort graduation rate. If the degree production ratio is valued at 15 percent, then the net price per FTE student is

Table 6.1. Regression Results for the Two-Year Price Model

Dependent variable: Net price per FTE student (in dollars)

Independent Variable	*Coefficient*	*Standard Error*
Constant	3331.27***	166.18
Degree production ratio (DPR)	1,298.04	691.75
Cohort graduation rate (CGR)	−2,547.04***	336.56
DPR × CGR	6,658.14***	1,806.78
Government appropriations as a percentage of core revenue (GA)	−2,302.21***	270.21
Local appropriations as a percentage of total government appropriations (LA)	−1,491.11***	265.74
GA × LA	1,967.29***	539.97
Underrepresented minorities as a percentage of total enrollment	−620.40***	108.53
Region		
West	−398.12***	47.35
South Central	−448.88***	53.32
North Central	29.46	41.89
South	−377.22***	41.87
New England	329.59***	72.51
Urban setting	85.66*	42.09

Notes: $N = 566$; $F = 82.15$***; $R^2 = .659$. See Exhibit 6.1 for variable definitions.
*$p < .05$; **$p < .01$; ***$p < .001$.

predicted to decrease by $15.48 for every 1 percent increase in the cohort graduation rate.

An actual example helps illustrate the interactive effect of the two variables. One of the colleges in the data set has a degree production ratio near 10 percent and reports a cohort graduation rate close to 10 percent as well. The campus is located in the South in an urban setting, and underrepresented minorities make up about 30 percent of the student population. Half of the school's core revenue derives from government funds, but only 1 percent of the government funding comes from the local community. The model predicts a net price per FTE student of $1,639. What would the model predict if the same institution doubled the degree production ratio to 20 percent while the cohort graduation rate remained at 10 percent—that is, if the college were in the degree business although it was not recording an efficient throughput rate? In that case, the predicted net price would be approximately $1,835 per FTE student, nearly $200 higher than the earlier figure. If the cohort graduation rate doubled (to 20 percent) but the degree ratio remained steady at 10 percent, the institution would be characterized as having a "boutique" credentialing operation. Net price per FTE would be predicted at $1,451, or $188 lower than the original estimate of $1,639. However, if both values doubled simultaneously, making the institution one that is primarily and successfully in the degree-granting business, the predicted net price would be $1,714, close to $75 more than the original predicted value.

A number of institutions fall in the middle of this spectrum of possibilities. They produce a moderate proportion of degrees and certificates relative to their size, and they graduate a moderate proportion of students who matriculated into certificate and associate degree programs. Institutions may be anomalous in that they have high degree production but a low graduation rate or low degree production and a high graduation rate, but few such cases occur.

Tuition is generally low at public two-year institutions, and government funds account for a healthy share of the revenue base. In the model, the more government money that goes to support an institution's core budget, the lower the net price per FTE student. One not necessarily expected but interesting finding is that at most levels of total appropriation, the larger the local share of government appropriations, the smaller the net price per FTE student. When appropriations reach three-quarters of core revenue—as happens in only roughly 2.5 percent of the cases—the effect of increasing the local share is essentially nil.

All other things being equal, net tuition revenue per FTE student is lower for institutions that serve a higher proportion of students from underrepresented minority populations. Whether this trend is the result of institutional efforts to expand access by keeping the stated price lower, because these colleges are providing more institutional aid to minority students, or because the institutions have less expensive and in that sense less robust education programs, the outcome is the same: lower tuition revenue.

Finally, setting matters too. All other things being equal, urban institutions accumulate, on average, $85 more net tuition revenue per FTE student than suburban or rural institutions. Similarly, a school in New England will average more net tuition revenue per FTE student than a comparable school in any other region of the country. Regional economic differences appear to play a role in determining price.

Creating and Testing Three Distinct Segments

Given the parallel in the price models between the two- and four-year markets, can the degree production ratio play a segment-defining role for the public community college market in the same way that completion rates do in segmenting the baccalaureate market? Such a finding would suggest that American higher education is less differentiated in terms of price and program than previously assumed and that there may be a single market reality underlying the pricing policies and practices pursued by most institutions of higher education. Such a finding would have the added benefit of yielding a dependable market-segmenting measure that derives from two very reliable data elements: enrollment and degrees or certificates awarded in a given year.

In fact, the degree production ratio provides a viable criterion for partitioning the community college market into three definable market segments. This fits neatly with our previous analysis of the "user-friendly" segment among four-year colleges, and when it proved significant in the model (including its interaction with the cohort graduation rate), we verified that it would provide clear breaks. (We also tested the cohort graduation rate as an alternative basis for classification. It did not work quite as well, nor were we entirely comfortable using a variable that depends heavily on an institution's definition of an initial cohort.)

Finding the segment boundaries began with a process of splitting the initial set of colleges into a series of small, overlapping data sets based on the value of the degree production ratio. By charting changes in the value of the coefficients of the other independent variables as we ran the model using the newly created overlapping data sets, it was possible to note where there were dramatic turns and shifts. Two cut points—at degree ratios of 10 percent and 15 percent—were clear places where the coefficients shifted, either peaking or reaching a minimum. These cuts divided the set of 644 institutions with sufficient data to calculate a degree production ratio roughly into thirds, yielding three market segments, which we call degree focus, mixed focus, and course focus. Degree focus—consisting of institutions that concentrate in programs that lead to degrees—was the smallest segment with just under 30 percent of the institutions. The largest market segment, comprising nearly 40 percent of the 644 classifiable institutions, were those whose primary focus appeared to be the delivery of courses—whether or not they were part of a degree program. For that reason we labeled this segment "course focus." The mixed focus segment, combining elements of both degree and course focus, constituted the third segment, accounting for roughly a third of the institutions in the analysis.

The Ordering of Two-Year Market Segments

Cohort graduation rate, price per FTE enrollment, percent part-time faculty, and other institutional characteristics for each of the three segments of the two-year market are easily distinguished from one another in Figures 6.1 through 6.4. On the one end, the degree focus segment includes the lowest proportion of urban institutions, generally serves the smallest percentage of underrepresented minority students, and graduates the largest percentage of its cohort of degree-seekers (Figure 6.1).

The profile of the course focus segment is opposite that of the degree focus segment, while mixed focus institutions fall between the two. In addition, degree focus institutions have the lowest enrollments. The median enrollment at a degree focus institution is just over 2,000; at a mixed focus institution, it is just over 3,300. By comparison, more than half of the course focus institutions have enrollments exceeding 6,300, and over one-fourth enroll more than 10,900 students.

Figure 6.1. Selected Institutional Characteristics by Market Segment

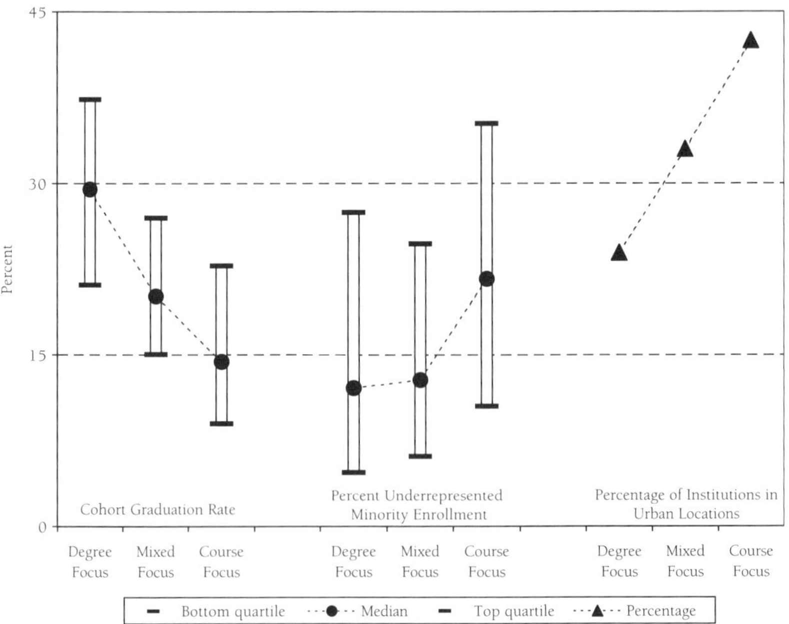

Any model, taxonomy, or classification system is useful only to the extent that it yields a better understanding of how the entities being analyzed perform. One of the key aspects of the two-year price model, in addition to its ability to predict price, is the fact that a variety of important indicators are aligned across its market segments. Even the *calculated* price (defined as net tuition revenue plus government appropriations divided by FTE students) tracks across the price model's three segments. Thus *both* calculated price, which includes the public subsidy, and net price, which does not include the public subsidy, track monotonically across the three segments. On average, two-year colleges in the degree focus segment have the most resources per FTE enrollment; institutions in the course focus segment have the least. The difference in the mean calculated price per FTE student across segments is statistically significant ($p < .05$) (see Figure 6.2).

Other characteristics are ordered across market segment as well. Degree focus institutions employ a smaller percentage of part-time faculty and serve fewer part-time students (see Figure 6.3). While Degree Focus institutions are found to have the lowest average nine- and ten-month academic salaries, they tend to have the largest proportion of faculty on eleven- or twelve-month contracts. Curious as this finding may be, it suggests that there are underlying structural differences in how institutions in each segment employ faculty, probably related to issues of unionization and bargaining for which there are not sufficient data to include in the model (see Figure 6.4).

Figure 6.2. Calculated Price per FTE Enrollment by Market Segment

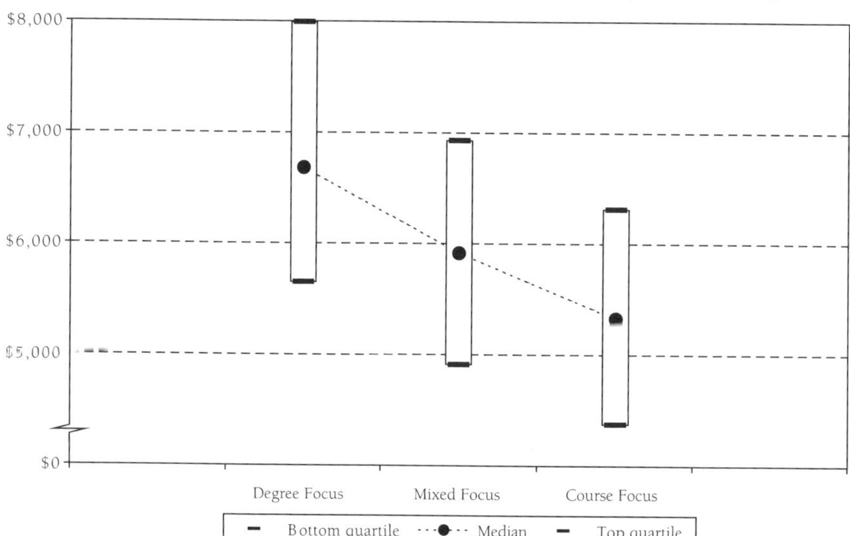

Figure 6.3. Percent Part-Time Faculty and Students by Market Segment

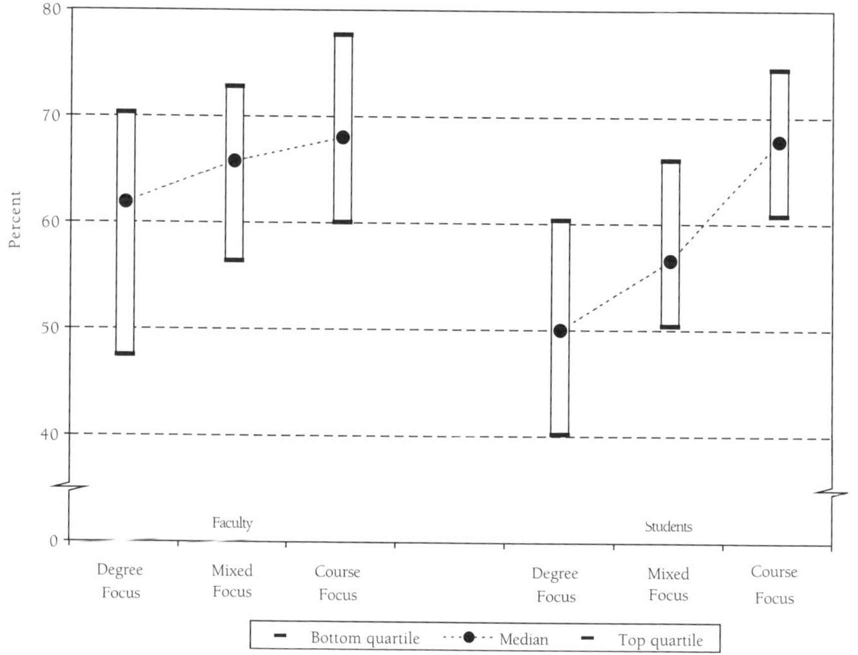

Figure 6.4. Faculty Salary* by Market Segment and Percent of Institutions with at Least Some 11/12 Month Salaries

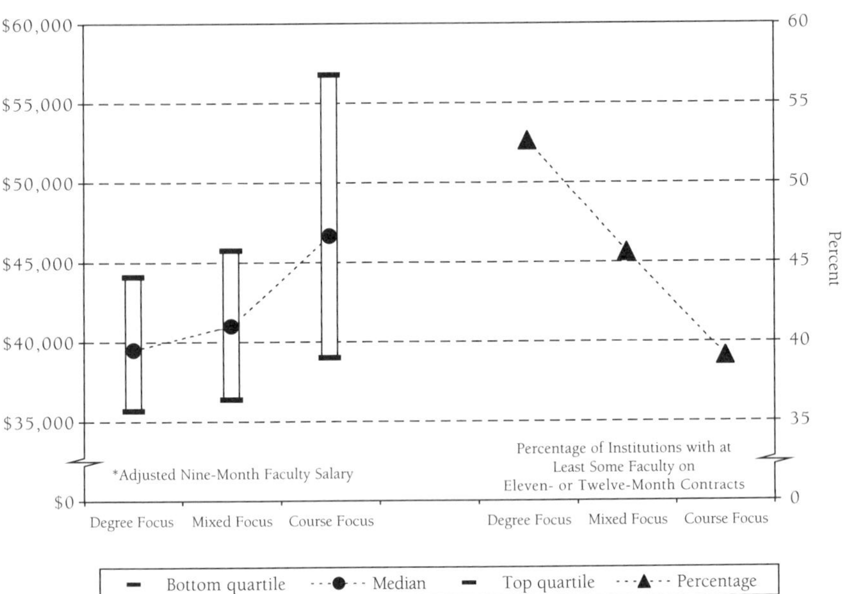

Finally, it is interesting to note that the percentage of part-time faculty is highest at course focus institutions, and the average faculty salary is highest at these institutions as well. Such findings suggest at least the possibility that institutions in this segment use additional part-time faculty in order to afford higher salaries for their full-time faculty.

When Two-Year Markets Matter

Most observers will be surprised that the market for community colleges is so neatly ordered, seemingly little different in its structure from the market for baccalaureate institutions. A few may want to argue that these results are misleading. "Is it truly a market," they will want to ask, "when choice is limited because most customers are place-bound?" Those who know the intricacies individual states use to finance community colleges may well want to ask, "Is it truly a market when some states set uniform fees?" What the power of the price model suggests, however, is that students who choose to enroll in a two-year institution do, in fact, have alternatives. While a convenient location is undoubtedly a powerful draw for many and perhaps even most students who chose to enroll in a two-year institution, other salient factors also come into play. Does the institution offer the courses or programs the student wants? At convenient times? Will the institution accept credits from other institutions? Will credits earned transfer easily to another institution? Does the institution provide appropriate remediation and academic support? And of course, can the student save some money by taking courses at one college rather than another? Even when the fees are relatively uniform across institutions, revenue per student may not be—and that, in the final analysis, is the definition of price the model uses.

It may be that the price that two-year institutions charge is not as much a function of the competition among two-year institutions as it is a function of the competition between two- and four-year institutions. From this perspective, the community college sector is not separate, not walled off, but in reality an integral part of the larger market for postsecondary education—a market in which price does matter and reflects the nature of the product as much as the interplay between supply and demand. To the extent that this latter observation holds true, the good news is that institutions can still determine their own future, deciding what to offer, when, and to whom. For community colleges to exercise that freedom, however, will require a more sustained appreciation of the workings of the market for postsecondary education in the United States and the role two-year institutions have actually come to play in that enterprise.

References

National Center for Postsecondary Improvement. "The User-Friendly Terrain: Defining the Market Taxonomy for Two-Year Institutions." *Change,* Jan.-Feb. 1998, pp. 35–38.

Zemsky, R, Shaman, S. M., and Shapiro, D. *Higher Education as Competitive Enterprise: When Markets Matter.* New Directions for Institutional Research, no. 111. San Francisco: Jossey-Bass, 2001.

SUSAN M. SHAMAN *was the University of Pennsylvania's director of institutional research for nearly twenty years and later its assistant vice president for planning analysis. She currently serves as senior research analyst for the Learning Alliance.*

ROBERT ZEMSKY *was the founding director of Penn's Institute for Research on Higher Education and currently serves as the chair and CEO of the Learning Alliance.*

Part Two

Reactions to the Proposed Models

7

The authors examine and discuss the utility of the classification systems proposed for community colleges from the perspective of the American Association of Community Colleges. Each proposed system has its strengths and limitations, and the discussion provides insights for understanding the differences among community colleges.

The Perspective of the American Association of Community Colleges

Kent A. Phillippe, George R. Boggs

The American Association of Community Colleges (AACC) is the primary advocacy organization for the nation's regionally accredited community colleges. Because timely information and data are essential to effective advocacy, AACC encourages any efforts that increase awareness of the complexities of community colleges and how they operate. However, AACC does not endorse any system of hierarchically ranking institutions or groups of institutions. Classification systems should not be designed as indicators of institutional quality but rather as tools to guide the study of community colleges. Valid and reliable research can inform policy development and legislation and can provide benchmarks needed to improve systems and institutions. Classification structures are useful instruments to frame analysis and to make fair comparisons. The classification systems presented in this publication reveal the complexities of trying to divide community colleges into categories that are both fair and useful.

Community colleges, like the rest of higher education, are difficult to quantify and therefore not easy to categorize. Governance systems for the colleges differ significantly by state, financing mechanisms can differ widely even within a state, and curriculum is usually distinct even for colleges in the same district. While many community colleges share the same core mission, the subtle and not so subtle differences between colleges, as well as the breadth of missions within some colleges, can be difficult to comprehend. The proposed classification systems outlined and discussed in Part One of this volume, which are intended to differentiate community colleges into distinct groupings, add to the understanding of these complex and multifaceted institutions.

While each of these proposals adds a different dimension to the understanding of community colleges, none is complete in and of itself. No single classification system seems to fit all situations. It is conceivable that a researcher might choose from among several classification systems, depending on the nature of the study. For example, an analysis of community college finances should probably use a classification system that includes local funding as a variable, whereas such a system might be less important in a study of program offerings.

Classification Factors Not Addressed in the Models

The distinction between publicly controlled institutions and those that are independent (for profit and not for profit) appears throughout these classification systems. AACC includes both public and independently controlled institutions in its membership and is interested in information affecting any of these colleges. However, the number of independently controlled colleges eligible for AACC membership is significantly smaller than that represented in the classification systems presented here. This difference is due primarily to AACC's requirement for regional accreditation for membership eligibility. In fact, AACC membership eligibility could itself be considered a classification system, as it limits the potential universe of institutional members to regionally accredited postsecondary institutions that offer an associate degree.

In determining eligibility for institutional membership in the association, the AACC constitution states that "membership is open to community, junior, and technical colleges and similar postsecondary institutions which offer an associate degree and are accredited by a regional accrediting association recognized by the Council on Higher Education Accreditation." By definition, this excludes a large number of colleges, both publicly and independently controlled, that are associate degree–granting institutions, although the majority of the excluded institutions are independently controlled. In addition, it opens membership to institutions that grant a baccalaureate or higher degree that also offer an associate degree and choose to identify themselves as a community college. In practice, few AACC member colleges offer a baccalaureate degree.

Given the association's unique definition of a community college, it is still important that both publicly and independently controlled institutions remain a part of any system to classify them, even though the association would prefer to limit it to regionally accredited colleges. As reflected in the AACC constitution, the role of regional accreditation is an important measure of academic standards that the AACC board of directors has determined useful for evaluating colleges for potential membership. It is one dimension that did not appear in any of the models presented in this publication.

One other important factor that is not considered in any of the models presented in this publication is the role of noncredit education in the college. This is a vital aspect of many institutions, accounting for as much as two-thirds of the enrollment at some institutions (Phillippe and Patton, 2000). Several authors did note the importance of noncredit education. However, they were unable to use this variable, stating that the lack of a consistent source of data on noncredit activity at the college precluded them from including it in their models. The closest any of the classification systems were to using this dimension was to discuss revenues from auxiliary sources as a potential proxy for noncredit revenues.

Commentary on the Classification Models

For a classification system to be effective, it must lead to a better understanding of the colleges in question, and it should provide a researcher or practitioner with groupings of colleges that are useful and meaningful. It is with this purpose in mind that we offer our comments on the various models and schemes proposed in Part One.

Stephen Katsinas provides a model that is driven to a large extent by the geographical context as well as the governance structure of the college. This model, like the Merisotis and Shedd model, divides the colleges first into publicly and independently controlled institutions. One of the strengths of this model is the utility it provides to individuals interested in state-level policy analysis. Because it differentiates the large multicampus or multicollege institutions from large single-campus colleges, it is also useful for research on institutional structures, dynamics, and leadership. The organizational structure of a multicollege district is likely to be quite distinct from that of a single-campus college, making this differentiation important for understanding these governance structures.

The Katsinas model does not, however, include any measure of local funding as a source of revenue for the college. For policy purposes, this is a critical factor that can drive many state and local decisions. Colleges with significant local revenues can be somewhat sheltered from the impact of state financial crises. For example, a 5 percent cut in state revenues has a bigger impact for a college that receives half of its funds from state sources than it has for a college that receives only one-third of its revenue from the state.

A review of the categorization of independently controlled colleges in the Katsinas model shows that distinctions made are less fine-grained than those used in the public sector, leading to larger sets of colleges in several of the groupings (720 and 595 in the two largest). To provide more utility in analyzing these colleges, a finer level of distinction would be useful. For example, programmatic offerings, such as those used by Merisotis and Shedd, could prove a useful means for differentiating the "special-use institutions."

The Katsinas model is somewhat unique in this volume in that it did not directly include any measure of academic or curricular activity for differentiating the publicly controlled colleges. Instead, this model relies on geographical location (urban, suburban, or rural), enrollment size, and governance as proxies for this activity. Enrollment was a key variable in many of the other models, even those that focus on academic or curricular activities.

In the chapter by Gwyer Schuyler, the percentage of liberal arts courses offered by public community colleges was the driving force for designing a model to differentiate colleges. An ideal model was developed that differentiated the colleges by size and percentage of English courses provided. However, since the percentage of English classes is not readily available for all colleges, the final model provided a two-level classification plan based strictly on enrollment (based on observed correlations between enrollment and curriculum characteristics).

The initial intent of this model—to look at liberal arts courses as a proxy for type of instructional programming—provides a good context for looking at the type of educational activity in which the college is engaged. Colleges that have a predominant focus on vocational programs and workforce development can differ significantly from those that focus primarily on academic transfer curricula. Differentiating colleges by the type of courses offered can lead to a richer understanding of the differences between colleges.

Unfortunately, the level of detail required for this classification plan is not universally available for community colleges. Therefore, the model relies on enrollment as a proxy for curricular offerings, allowing a differentiation of colleges into only two groupings. The use of only two categories of colleges significantly reduces the utility of the model as an analytic tool.

Arthur Cohen argues for an enrollment-based classification system for public community colleges. He makes the case that overall enrollment is related to many other dimensions that are important to understanding community colleges, such as instructional expenditures as a percentage of total education and general expenditures, percentage of faculty who are full-time, and percentage of revenue from auxiliary sources. However, since the variables mentioned are readily available from IPEDS, using the actual variables rather than enrollment as a proxy may be a better choice.

The classification plan proposed by Cohen suggests dividing the public community colleges into small, medium, and large colleges. An equal distribution of colleges into thirds would result in roughly 300+ colleges per category. However, this somewhat arbitrary division based on equal proportions could easily mask important underlying differences among these colleges.

The chapter by Merisotis and Shedd uses the complex analytic tool of cluster analysis to develop college categories. Yet in the end, the public colleges are split according to enrollment—an approach not significantly different from that proposed by Cohen.

The methodology that Merisotis and Shedd use to develop their categories is instructive, however. The variables of interest for developing the models were those frequently associated with different aspects of community college missions, such as urbanicity, ratio of degrees to certificates, percentage of classes in occupationally specific programs, and percentage of education and general expenditures on instruction.

The analysis provided sufficient evidence to indicate that the publicly and independently controlled colleges need to be analyzed separately. Like the previous models, enrollment proved to be the tool that separated the publicly controlled community colleges most efficiently into distinct groups. And as in the Cohen and Schuyler chapters, these categories proved to be related to differences in the other variables. Therefore, although the categories were based on enrollments, the description of each grouping is based on the tendencies of these colleges to be similar with regard to the other variables included in the analysis. Unfortunately, the model was unable to use noncredit activity for these colleges and did not use local funding as a variable in the analysis. Inclusion of these factors might have provided a different and more comprehensive view of these colleges.

For the independently controlled colleges in the Merisotis and Shedd model, programmatic completions were an important driving force in differentiating the colleges. In the not-for-profit sector, a unique group of colleges offered allied health programs exclusively, and these were therefore separated from the rest of the colleges. The single-mission institution is in line with the concept of "specialized" institutions introduced by Katsinas. The for-profit sector, on the other hand, was easily split, based on the level of awards predominantly offered—certificates of less than two years versus two-year degrees. The ability to differentiate these colleges on the basis of programmatic variables has appeal, as it is closer than enrollment to identifying what is core to the college's mission.

Like the Cohen and Schuyler proposals, categorizing the publicly controlled colleges based on enrollment alone seems to provide less useful categories for analytic purposes. It is true that enrollment is related to many other variables of importance. The problem with adopting this scheme as a categorical tool is that others might infer that changing a college's enrollment could result in a change in the related variables.

Shaman and Zemsky take a different approach to categorizing the community colleges. Rather than starting with an institutional frame of reference, the model uses a market- or student-based framework. In other words, what is it about the price or cost of attendance that can be used to differentiate the colleges?

The model's use of financial variables (such as local appropriations as a percentage of all government appropriations), geographical variables (such as region and urbanicity), and outcome measures (such as cohort graduation rates) provides a useful conceptual framework within which to view community colleges. The resulting model provides a useful tool for looking at community colleges relative to other higher education institutions in the "market." However, one methodological concern about this model is that one dependent variable (degrees awarded divided by total enrollment) in the regression analysis that had marginal predictive significance ($p < .06$) was the variable used for differentiating the categories.

In addition, this model does not include any academic or programmatic information other than degree production and cohort graduation rates. Although these might be useful for the researcher interested in such outcomes, it is not the goal of many community college students. Therefore, colleges with low cohort graduation rates and low degree production might be negatively viewed relative to their counterparts when they may in fact be serving their constituencies equally effectively.

As with the other models, noncredit activity is also not included in this model, and this exclusion could have significant implications for a price-based model. For example, a student may have the option of taking the same course for credit or noncredit. The price difference at this college (cost for a credit course versus the cost for a noncredit course) might be a stronger deciding factor than the relative price difference between this college and another college. However, a similar student at a different community college in a different state may not have a credit or noncredit option for the same course.

Conclusion

With the exception of the Shaman and Zemsky model, size appears to be the most important factor that drives the proposed categorization systems of the public community colleges. In fact, size is predominantly used as a utilitarian tool or proxy for differentiating the colleges along the many other dimensions of interest. However, the resulting college categories are relatively large, allowing an analyst to make finer distinctions, according to the policy or research question of interest, based on other factors. The Katsinas model made some of those distinctions, which would prove useful for certain policy-related questions or for studying organizational structures and complexities.

The Shaman and Zemsky model, by contrast, suggests that student choice is the key driving force and that institutional differences can be discerned in the market forces that drive students to make different choices. This methodological framework has a lot of appeal for policymakers. However, the complex nature of students' behavior that affects their choice in attending the community college needs to be further understood before this model will have face validity with many in the community college field.

The institution's community context is a critical factor for consideration in classification. Urbanicity is used in several of the models to address geographical location. However, this is a proxy for the more subtle factors underlying these higher-level classifications. For example, the economic base, and thus the nature of the college's vocational education offerings, differs even in communities considered to be in similar geographical settings. The combination of region and urbanicity provides more insight but still does little to address the important contextual factors that forge a community college's identity.

Each of the classification systems proposed by the authors has both strengths and limitations. Grouping community colleges is difficult. The missions are ostensibly similar, but the institutions serve the educational needs of people in diverse communities with often different expectations, and they operate within different governance structures. Community colleges are also known for their responsiveness to local needs and their entrepreneurial culture, both of which can lead to shifts in the balance of the curriculum and even changes in funding. Despite these difficulties, it is important to develop frameworks to guide research and analysis. The authors provide a basis for guiding further discussion and development.

Reference

Phillippe, K. A., and Patton, M. (eds.). *National Profile of Community Colleges: Trends and Statistics.* (3rd ed.) Washington, D.C.: Community College Press, 2000.

KENT A. PHILLIPPE is the senior research associate at the American Association of Community Colleges, where he has worked for nearly a decade. He has written several publications on community college trends and statistics and serves on many national educational research advisory panels.

GEORGE R. BOGGS served as a faculty member, division chair, and associate dean of instruction at Butte College in Oroville, California, and was for fifteen years the superintendent and president of Palomar College in San Marcos, California. He is currently the president and CEO of the American Association of Community Colleges in Washington, D.C.

8

Each scheme described in the first part of this volume has strengths and weaknesses, which are identified and discussed in this chapter.

A Practitioner's Perspective

Alfredo G. de los Santos Jr.

The authors of the chapters in Part Two of this volume were asked to respond to the classification schemes outlined in Part One. The respondents were provided with a set of questions and asked to address them but not necessarily to limit comments to them. These questions were as follows: Would the various schemes be useful to you in your work? How might they be improved? Are there important dimensions of variation that none of the schemes get at? How might we get at them? How important is it to include or exclude private institutions from a classification scheme? What unintended consequences might result from the adoption and proliferation of one or more of these classification schemes?

The authors of the schemes suggest important criteria for a classification system. Arthur Cohen writes in Chapter Four that "the resulting information must be descriptive but not hierarchical," that the criteria used in the scheme "must be *valid*," that the "data used in a classification scheme must be *readily available*," and that the "categories must be *readily understandable*" (emphasis added). Katsinas, after doing a careful analysis of the Carnegie classifications, outlines in Chapter Two the three key factors that "helped Kerr's classification scheme become widely accepted": objective data from nationally recognized sources, criteria deemed meaningful by users, and stable classification groupings. In Chapter Five, Merisotis and Shedd suggest five criteria. The first is that the data must be collected at the national level. The classification system must also be replicable and must have "a manageable number of categories." They add that "each institution should reside in only one category." In other words, the categories must be mutually exclusive. The classification system "must make policy-relevant distinctions among institutions." Finally, the categories must be "descriptive and not evaluative or hierarchical."

Generally, a combination of the criteria suggested by these authors and my own experience over more than thirty-five years as a community college executive in four states were used to vet the utility of the classification systems described. The chapters in Part One of the book were studied, and each classification scheme was carefully reviewed. Then a list of the criteria or descriptors for classification scheme suggested by the authors was prepared. I then reread each chapter and analyzed each of the proposed systems. The criteria applied included whether the schemes are valid, meaningful, descriptive and not hierarchical, replicable, mutually exclusive, policy-relevant, and suitable for use with readily available objective data collected regularly at the national level.

Katsinas's System

The criteria proposed by Katsinas (Chapter Two)—institutional control, governance, geography, and size—and the application of these criteria to classify community colleges produce an interesting array of groupings and categories. The groupings suggested seem to fit a number of the criteria that might be used in devising a system for classifying community colleges. The data are objective and are collected nationally on a regular basis, and the groupings are mutually exclusive. The system is descriptive and not hierarchical; it is valid; and it can be replicated. Finally, the system makes sense and has meaning, at least for this author.

The classification system suggested by Katsinas offers interesting groupings, in comparison to the other schemes suggested in this volume. However, some further work and analysis should be considered. The "multicampus" category raises questions. Are there differences between a multicollege district in which each college is separately accredited (for example, the Maricopa County Community College District or the Dallas County Community College District) and one accredited college that has multiple campuses (for example, Miami-Dade Community College or Pima Community College)?

Over the years, for example, in some reports, Miami-Dade Community College has been referred to as "the largest community college" in the country. Technically this is correct; it is the *one* college with the largest enrollment in its several campuses. But the Dallas and Maricopa districts are indeed larger if the total enrollment of *all* of their colleges is considered. It is not clear what the policy implications of this are, but the questions remain.

Katsinas argues that the use of the term *urbanicity* in the NCES's IPEDS system is value-laden and might have negative implications for the smaller rural colleges. Perhaps it is because I spent twenty-one years serving as a vice chancellor in the largest community college district in the country, the Maricopa County Community College District, but the negative connotations are not clear at all.

Merisotis and Shedd's IPEDS-Based Scheme

Merisotis and Shedd (Chapter Five) use the IPEDS data to develop a classification system for two-year colleges and suggest institutional control as one of the criteria. In effect, they suggest three categories of institutional control for the colleges: public, private not-for-profit, and private for-profit. Although they did not include the other category suggested by Katsinas (federally chartered and special-use institutions), I agree with the three categories they suggest. However, adding the fourth category suggested by Katsinas would enhance this scheme.

Using the three categories of institutional control, they then analyzed IPEDS data and created three "distinguishable categories" for public two-year colleges, two categories for private not-for-profit institutions, and two for private for-profit institutions.

The classification system they developed is interesting and meets many of the criteria I outlined. However, it does not meet two or three important ones, the first one being that the system must be *meaningful*. To be frank, it is easy to get lost in the names assigned to the each of the categories, and it is difficult to understand the full utility of the categories created.

Beyond that, one could argue that their system might be interpreted as going beyond being descriptive and is hierarchical. For example, Merisotis and Shedd point out that the community megaconnector institutions have the "highest median percentage of part-time students enrolled (69 percent)" and the highest median percentage of part-time faculty (69 percent)." Some policymakers (and some groups of faculty) might interpret this in a negative way, given the general bias in favor of full-time faculty.

In addition, while they indicate that "an emphasis was placed on creating names that were not value-laden," one could argue otherwise. For example, in *community megaconnector institution,* the prefix *mega-* could suggest not only "extremely large" or "indicating a multiple of one million" but also, "extraordinary." Thus *mega-* might be interpreted by some as larger or better or more outstanding than mere *community connector institutions.*

Cohen's Scheme

The classification scheme outlined by Cohen (Chapter Four) uses the size of the community college—really, the number of students enrolled—as a fundamental criterion. Cohen related institutional size to other variables: percentages of full-time and part-students and faculty, percentage of revenue received from federal government grants and contracts, and per capita expenditures on instruction, using data readily available through IPEDS. His analysis yields interesting findings and groupings of institutions that have some utility in classifying two-year colleges.

In my view, using institutional enrollment—the size of the community college—as one of the criteria of a classification system is a must.

However, grouping two-year institutions according to the percentage of full-time and part-time faculty might have little utility in a policy setting. For example, in Arizona, there is no significant difference between the larger urban colleges and the smaller rural community colleges in terms of full-time and part-time faculty and students (State Board of Directors for Community Colleges of Arizona, 2001). This might be true in other states as well.

Cohen also advocates for the use of curriculum (really, the number of course sections offered) as a criterion in any scheme to classify community colleges while acknowledging that the data are not readily available nationally. Thus, although the use of the number of sections offered by instructional type (transfer, occupational, developmental) might yield important policy-relevant findings, it is not possible to use this as a criterion on a national level until and unless the NCES collects this information regularly. (For more on this, see my discussion of Schuyler's proposal.)

Shaman and Zemsky's Price Model

The classification scheme by Shaman and Zemsky (Chapter Six) is derived from a similar project they did for four-year colleges and universities. They use a different definition of *net price* for community colleges than they used for four-year colleges and universities: tuition and fees revenues minus institutional financial aid divided by FTE enrollment. They find that the model they developed "is robust, is intuitively satisfying, and accounts for a considerable fraction—nearly two-thirds—of the variance in net price per FTE student."

The difficulty with the model is that it might not be considered valid by some people in community colleges and might not be understood by others. The reason that some will not think the model valid is because some of the concepts or elements of the model, like "degree production ratio" and "cohort graduation rates," are not part of the daily vocabulary used in community colleges. Cohen, for example, in advocating that the criteria used for a classification scheme should be valid, notes some measures that are useless. And he includes "degrees awarded as a percentage of enrollment" as something that is not "useful to compute."

Another problem with the model is the definition of *net price*. The tuition and fees charged by community colleges across the country vary so much that to some observers, the use of this as an element of the model might be misunderstood. For example, the average in-state tuition and fees in 1997–98 for the ten states with the largest community college enrollment ranged from a high in New York of $2,576 to a low of $379 in California (ERIC Clearinghouse for Community Colleges, 2000).

Local governing boards and state boards agonize when they consider increasing the tuition and fees for community colleges. They never take into consideration notions like degree production ratio or cohort graduation rate. The issues that they discuss center on access, affordability, and the impact that the increases will have on the citizens that the community college is intended to serve.

Schuyler's Curriculum-Based Scheme

Gwyer Schuyler's analysis (Chapter Three) confirms the findings of prior work done at the UCLA Center for the Study of Community Colleges (CSCC) that community colleges do offer different proportions of transfer and occupational education programs. Thus using such a system would classify community colleges in terms of their emphasis on the type of instructional program.

However, this system has a number of problems, the most fundamental being the data: the data needed are not readily available and are difficult to obtain. Referring to the earlier CSCC studies, Schuyler notes that the data were compiled "through a time-consuming process of collecting, analyzing, and coding college course schedules" and notes that the "method is not practical." Instead, she suggests that a "viable and meaningful classification model can be designed with readily available data acting as proxies for curricular characteristics," including those that correlated with "percent liberal arts." However, the use of proxies may introduce problems.

Beyond that, some of the findings or groupings might engender invidious comparisons between types of institutions. For example, Schuyler found that the "percentage of expenditures that go toward instructional costs is a negative predictor of the percentage of liberal arts courses, meaning that the greater the percentage of expenditures that go toward instructional costs, the less the percentage of liberal arts courses in the curriculum. *In other words, colleges typically spend more per student in occupational programs*" (emphasis added).

In periods when fiscal resources are limited (as in the present), a community college that offers a higher percentage of occupational programs might feel pressure to reduce these offerings as a method of balancing the budget. During the recession of the 1980s, for example, one of the board members in the Maricopa Community Colleges asked for the cost per full-time-equivalent (FTE) student for each of the colleges and asked that this information be used in the decision-making process as the budget for the subsequent year was being developed.

The one college that offered the highest percentage of occupational programs in the district also happened to have a smaller total student enrollment. Given this, the cost per FTE student at this college was the highest in the district. The cost per FTE student at one of the larger colleges, whose occupational program offerings represented a smaller percentage of its total curricular offerings, was much lower—in fact, among the lowest in comparison with the other campus-based colleges. The president of that college at the time developed a brochure showing the per-student cost comparison of all the district colleges, with his having one of the lowest. Some people in the district inferred from this that this one college was more efficient and more effective than the smaller college with the larger occupational offering—an unfortunate comparison that caused more harm than good.

The overall utility of this scheme seems to be limited. What policy issues would be informed by this classification system? How would institutional leaders use this information? If a small college has a larger percentage of occupational programs than liberal arts programs, what are its options? To reduce the occupational programs and by so doing limiting its service to the community? If a larger college has a relatively small percentage of its offerings in occupational programs, will it try to compensate by reducing its liberal arts programs?

Conclusion

Of the schemes described and proposed in this volume, the one suggested by Katsinas meets the largest number of the criteria I used to vet the systems. This scheme, perhaps with some additional work and perhaps with some elements from the other models, might have the best utility. It is clear that a system to classify community colleges in this country is needed, both to inform policy and to shape the debate about the future of these institutions, which have become such an important part of our nation's educational system.

References

ERIC Clearinghouse for Community Colleges. *Community College Enrollment and Costs.* Los Angeles: ERIC Clearinghouse, 2000.

State Board of Directors for Community Colleges of Arizona. *Statistical Supplement to the Annual Report to the Governor, FY 2001–2002.* Phoenix: State Board of Directors for Community Colleges of Arizona, 2001.

ALFREDO G. DE LOS SANTOS JR. is a research professor at Arizona State University and a Senior League Fellow at the League for Innovation in the Community College.

9

The diversity of community colleges justifies a more subtle system of categorization than the traditional Carnegie system, but the large number of missions taken on by community colleges complicates this goal. Any system must be based on a clear understanding of the goals of the categorization. This chapter makes a distinction between a characteristics-based system and an output-based system and uses that distinction to discuss the proposed classification schemes.

A Researcher's Perspective

Thomas R. Bailey

Community colleges enroll a substantial proportion of all of the higher education students in the United States. These colleges accounted for 28 percent of all postsecondary students enrolled in October 1973 and 40 percent of the same group in 2000 (Carnegie Commission on Higher Education, 1973; Carnegie Foundation for the Advancement of Teaching, 2001). If one counts the total number of students enrolled in college over the course of a calendar year, the community college share rises to over 50 percent. And older individuals, returning to college to upgrade their skills or change careers, are much more likely to enroll in a two-year than a four-year school (Bailey and others, 2003). Community colleges also account for 42 percent of all institutions of higher education (Carnegie Foundation for the Advancement of Teaching, 2001). Two-year colleges are diverse, ranging from isolated rural institutions enrolling a few hundred students to gigantic urban colleges with tens of thousands of students taking classes at many different campuses and satellite sites. Community colleges also vary dramatically with respect to governance, finance, educational philosophy, and many other characteristics.

Despite the importance and extreme heterogeneity of community colleges, the Carnegie classification system, which has eighteen categories, lumps all community colleges into one group. Community colleges therefore get 5 percent of the categories even though they account for more than 40 percent of the institutions and the students. The simplistic view of community colleges embedded in the traditional classification system reflects a broader neglect of the sector in the research and policy communities. Only a small number of researchers, several of whom are represented in this collection, have devoted themselves to the serious study of the community college. Higher education policy discussions are much more likely to be focused on issues of concern to four-year colleges and universities. Thus this effort to develop a more sophisticated classification system is well warranted and long overdue.

Although the need for a more nuanced system is almost self-evident, there is less consensus about the purposes of that system. The choice of any classification scheme will depend fundamentally on the purposes to which it will be put. The chapters in Part One reveal a variety of classification goals. For example, Susan Shaman and Robert Zemsky (Chapter Six) develop a system that can be used to predict the prices charged by colleges. Steve Katsinas (Chapter Two) would like a system that serves several goals including benchmarking either for evaluation or for program improvement, facilitating sampling for research projects, helping researchers who have little concrete knowledge about community colleges, and providing guidance in the education of community college administrators and faculty. Jamie Merisotis and Jessica Shedd (Chapter Five) argue that a classification system can provide guidance in allocating funds, comparing institutional inputs and outputs, and making decisions about faculty, students, and staff. Gwyer Schuyler (Chapter Three) would like a system to differentiate between colleges that "focus on a liberal arts education (leading to transfer to baccalaureate-granting institutions) and those specializing in occupational training (leading to direct employment)." And while Arthur Cohen (Chapter Four) does not explicitly state the goals of a classification system, he is looking for a parsimonious approach that imparts the maximum amount of information with the least burdensome data-gathering requirements. In addition, he wants a system that does not allow normative comparisons between colleges and that is based on valid and meaningful criteria.

Approaches to Classification

The underlying philosophy and theory of classification is a complex science, and there are many types of classification systems. The system for classifying plants and animals, beloved to every tenth-grade biology student, is one of the most common and most influential. This system groups animals, for example, by their characteristics, although the groupings also have a basis in the evolution of those characteristics.

In contrast to this characteristics-based system, the system used to classify establishments or firms in the economy is based on the products produced by those establishments. This is called the Standard Industrial Classification (SIC) system and is based on a hierarchical categorization in which large classes, such as nondurable manufacturing or retail trade, are subdivided into smaller categories such as textiles or eating and drinking places. Establishments are assigned to these categories and subcategories based on their primary product or service without regard to their size, location, or ownership status.

Examples of both characteristics-based and outcomes-based systems can be found in this book. Merisotis and Shedd, Katsinas, and Cohen group colleges on the basis of important characteristics. Shaman and Zemsky and particularly Schuyler propose schemes that emphasize outputs. Schuyler's approach tries to differentiate between colleges that emphasize transfer from those that are more focused on terminal occupational degrees. Although Shaman and Zemsky start out in a search for a model to help predict prices, in the end their classification system differentiates between colleges that emphasize degrees and those that teach skills through individual courses.

Which type of classification system—one based on characteristics or one based on outputs—would be more appropriate for community colleges? This will of course depend on the goals of the system, so perhaps it makes sense to have a variety of systems, as the Carnegie Foundation is in fact planning to propose.

Challenges with Output-Based Classification

An output-based system has an intuitive appeal, especially if we think of higher education in general and community colleges in particular as industries that use inputs to produce products. From this perspective, it makes sense to compare colleges that are producing the same product. For example, consider two colleges, both of which emphasize liberal arts and transfer but one of which is a small college in a rural area and the other of which is a large college in an urban area. Certainly for many purposes, grouping colleges on the basis of the types of "products" they produce makes sense.

Moreover, historically, the Carnegie system is an output-based system. One of its strengths was that it gave a sense of the institutional mission of the colleges. Thus in the past, it was based on categorizations of two fundamental missions of higher education—the education of students as measured by the degrees that they are working toward and completing and the production of knowledge and research. For the most recent revision of the system in 2000, however, the research component was dropped, for several reasons. The data on which it was based were no longer available, and the measure itself gave a distorted and incomplete view of the research function of the institutions.

This diversity of classification objectives and frameworks for community colleges reflects two problems. First, whatever the theoretical goals of the classification system, data may not be easily available that would allow the development of that system. Therefore, an output-oriented scheme may end up looking like a characteristics-based approach. This is what happened with Schuyler's scheme. I will return to this practical problem later.

The second and deeper problem that thwarts the development of an outcomes-based system for community colleges is their diversity of mission. Community college administrators and faculty articulate several central college missions, including granting degrees, transfer, workforce development, worker upgrading, and remediation. (For a discussion of the forces that lead community colleges to take on many missions, see Bailey and Morest, 2003.) No strong national consensus has emerged that identifies one or two central purposes of the community college. This contrasts to views about four-year colleges. They are first and foremost bachelor's degree–granting institutions. For some of those colleges and universities, the production of knowledge and research is an additional widely accepted core mission. Service is often seen as a third mission, and failure to measure it is a common criticism of the Carnegie system, but in practice it is subordinate to the other missions. Moreover, even in comparison to research, the bachelor's degree production mission is paramount in the sense that no college president will try to argue that graduation rates are low *because* the institution focuses on research. To be sure, scholars debate whether the extreme focus on research in some institutions damages undergraduate education, but those who advocate research counter that the presence of research actually enhances undergraduate education. No one argues that a classification system needs to downgrade the importance of degree completion for research-oriented institutions (or service-oriented institutions).

If we had a consensus that the community college was first and foremost an associate degree–producing institution and that it did not have an important research role, then the current classification system and the category to which it assigns community colleges would be consistent and internally coherent, although one obvious amendment that would be consistent with the 2000 revisions would be to differentiate among two-year colleges based on the ratio of liberal arts to occupational degrees offered.

But there is no consensus that all other community college goals are clearly subordinate to the production of associate degree graduates. There are three broad reasons for this, and each stands in contrast to the role of the bachelor's degree in four-year institutions.

First, as Cohen points out, many students transfer to a four-year college without completing a degree. Thus if a community college were entirely focused on transfer to baccalaureate programs, it could in principle be 100 percent successful without graduating a single student. There is no analogous situation at the bachelor's level. Students aspiring to higher levels of education must pass through the B.A.

Second, community college administrators and faculty often argue that many of their students do not want degrees. They enroll to learn specific skills and therefore do not need to spend the time and money required to complete a full degree. For these students, the colleges are not associate degree–producing institutions but rather skills- and knowledge-teaching institutions. Although it would certainly be possible for the staff at four-year institutions to make these same arguments, it is my sense that this is much less common. Some presidents may argue that their graduation rates are low because their students face many social, educational, and economic problems, not because the noncompleters are really getting what they want. Students seeking "skills" from a four-year college are more likely to be enrolled in the sometimes gigantic noncredit extension divisions of the colleges.

Third, community colleges engage in a wide variety of activities outside of the traditional credit and degree-oriented programs. These include noncredit instruction, customized training, adult basic education, ESL instruction, and local economic development activities. Increasingly, community colleges are moving up or down educational levels, getting involved with teaching high school students or developing bachelor's degree programs themselves. There is no consensus about the relationship of these functions to the community college mission. But many community college administrators, faculty, and board members see these as absolutely central activities inherent in the college's goal to serve the diverse needs of their local communities. Four-year institutions also engage in many of these types of activities, which might be considered part of their service mission; nevertheless, the service functions of the community college are considered more central to the missions of the community colleges than the four-year colleges. This is reflected partly in the more important role of local funding in the finances of the community colleges.

For all these reasons, community college administrators and faculty are reluctant to consider the production of associate degrees as the college's paramount mission, with all other missions playing a subordinate role. If this is not the primary mission of the college, then what should it be? Some of the classification systems presented in this book suggest some alternatives. Shaman and Zemsky classify colleges based on the skills-versus-credentials (associate degrees and certificates) distinction. Schuyler emphasizes occupational versus academic and transfer education but does not directly take account of degrees or credentials.

The other classification schemes suggested in this book are not explicitly based on college outputs, but the authors do list several outcomes that are correlated with their categories. For example, while Cohen's system is based on enrollment size, his categories also differentiate among colleges with different relative levels of federal grants and contracts and auxiliary revenue. These could be measures of the extent to which the colleges serve their communities in various ways outside of credit instruction. Size is also related to the proportion of full- and part-time students, which might also reflect distinctions between an emphasis on educating traditional-aged college students versus adults returning to college for skill upgrading or career change. And although the system proposed by Merisotis and Shedd is characteristics-based rather than output-based, it does also, in practice, differentiate colleges according to output or output-related measures. For example, these include the relative importance of certificates among the credentials given by the colleges, the relative number of full- (and first-time) and part-time students, and the importance of occupational versus academic (and transfer) programs.

Thus if we are looking for an output-based system, there are many possible outputs. Developing a parsimonious system will be difficult, in the absence of a consensus about the two or three most important aspects of these "products." Choosing to focus on particular outputs risks leaving out other central missions. For example, Shaman and Zemsky focus on the distinction between credentials and "skills" but do not consider transfer, the academic-versus-occupational split, or the broader community service college activities. Schuyler focuses on the academic-versus-occupational or transfer-versus-terminal split but not on degrees. A more complete measure might try to combine information about the degree type, transfer, and credentials and skills.

Challenges with Addressing Mission

A broad attempt to measure college missions would probably include some measures of the types and nature of the degrees or programs offered, measures of program features designed to teach skills and knowledge not captured by degree completion, and a variety of measures of an orientation toward broader community service. As I have argued, the contributors to Part One of this book have tried to get some of these features, but data availability has thwarted these efforts.

While Schuyler started to develop a system based on the academic-versus-occupational contrast, in the end her system simply relies on enrollment size, appealing to the correlation between enrollments and the ratio of general education to occupational courses. Shaman and Zemsky contrast a credential-versus-skills mission, but their classification measures combine the colleges' policy with their success in implementing that policy. That is, a college that wants to emphasize credentials but does a poor job of retaining students may be categorized as a college that "emphasizes skills."

Measuring a college's commitment to local community service is also difficult. The share of revenues from grants and contracts or from federal sources may reflect an emphasis in the college on addressing the needs of students with academic and social problems or on serving the community outside of the regular credit programs. The importance of local funding may also be a measure of this community service function. Unfortunately, these measures are influenced by state funding policies and often by local economic conditions, and they will therefore provide a distorted image of institutional emphasis on broader community service.

Note that the 2000 revisions of the Carnegie system in effect retreated to a measure that can be considered an indication of institutional policy and therefore, presumably, mission. Thus the system focused on the level of degree, the number of different types of degrees, and for baccalaureate colleges, the relative importance of liberal arts fields. The research component was eliminated because it was poorly related to an acceptable measure of the research mission.

Conclusion

Although each of the classification systems presented in this volume can be used to generate interesting and important insights, classification systems could be strengthened through the following steps. The purposes of the classification systems need to be much more systematically defined, and the link between those goals and the measures proposed need to be clearly articulated. As we have seen, the authors of the chapters in Part One articulate a variety of goals, although in some cases the link between those goals and the systems that they propose is not clear. But since different goals will in all likelihood be best served by different schemes, it makes sense either to propose a variety of systems or to provide easily available data that can be used to generate many systems. If we are looking for a system that can be used to benchmark practices, it will be different from one used to distribute money or to help select a sample of community colleges for a research project.

From the point of view of a researcher, a system that differentiates among the missions of colleges would be particularly useful. Researchers would like to be able to group and to compare institutions that are essentially performing the same functions. Only two of these schemes explicitly set out to do this, although the categories in some of the other systems may be correlated with various missions. And as we have seen, data availability makes this particularly difficult. But given this problem, I see some important benefits to efforts to develop a mission-oriented system.

First, as I have emphasized, there is no consensus about the paramount mission of the community college. By defining a set of missions and trying to measure them, any classification effort will lead to a useful discussion about the missions of the colleges. Indeed, I can imagine a variety of systems based on different understandings of college missions. These would be particularly useful if they included written discussion of the reasoning behind a particular emphasis on one or more missions.

Second, a classification system would be particularly useful for a researcher if it led to the development of data that are not currently available. A system based on easily available IPEDS data may be useful for the general public, but is not particularly important for researchers, who also have access to IPEDS and can therefore generate their own systems. But if the development of a mission-oriented system led to the collection of new data through IPEDS that would help define and measure college missions, the process would represent a significant advance for research.

All of the schemes suggested in this collection are useful because they illustrate the variety of purposes and approaches that can be taken in developing a classification system. But the case for each scheme could be strengthened, and the overall discussion advanced, if these authors explicitly articulated the goals of their system, why they chose those goals above others, and how actual operationalization of their system related to the goals with which they set out.

References

Bailey, T. R., and Morest, V. S. *The Organizational Efficiency of the Multiple Missions for Community Colleges.* New York: Community College Research Center, Teachers College, Columbia University, 2003.

Bailey, T. R., and others. "The Characteristics of Occupational Sub-Baccalaureate Students Entering the New Millennium." Paper prepared for the U.S. Department of Education National Assessment of Vocational Education, 2003.

Carnegie Commission on Higher Education. *A Classification of Institutions of Higher Education.* Berkeley, Calif.: Carnegie Commission on Higher Education, 1973.

Carnegie Foundation for the Advancement of Teaching. *The Carnegie Classification of Institutions of Higher Education, 2000 Edition.* Menlo Park, Calif.: Carnegie Foundation for the Advancement of Teaching, 2001.

THOMAS R. BAILEY is the George and Abbey O'Neil Professor of Economics and Education in the Department of International and Transcultural Studies at Teachers College, Columbia University. He directs both the Institute on Education and the Economy and the Community College Research Center at Teachers College.

Part Three

Classification in Practice

10

This concluding chapter illustrates the practical results of the five classification proposals. Each classification model has been applied to a common sample of colleges, and the authors review the key implications of this collective exercise.

Classification in Practice: Applying Five Proposed Classification Models to a Sample of Two-Year Colleges

Rebecca D. Cox, Alexander C. McCormick

In the interest of presenting a practical illustration of the five proposed classification models, each was applied to a randomly-selected set of two-year colleges. The resulting categorizations are presented in Exhibits 10.1 through 10.6, and offer the opportunity to compare and contrast the way each classification scheme arrays the colleges.

Exhibit 10.1 provides an overview of the five proposals, identifying the actual classifications that individual colleges would receive under each of the five schemes. In conjunction with the other exhibits in this chapter, which display the distinct groupings that result from each proposal, it illuminates additional practical complications of the classification enterprise. The intent is to provide a concrete illustration of the proposed models, calling attention to points of convergence and divergence, thereby suggesting directions for further conceptualization and refinement. This chapter summarizes several issues that have emerged in this analysis.

The set of 114 colleges selected for this exercise is a sample of public and private degree-granting Title IV–eligible two-year colleges drawn from the Integrated Postsecondary Education Data System (IPEDS) of the U.S. Department of Education's National Center for Education Statistics. These 80 public and 34 private colleges comprise a common sample for putting each classification model into practice. Exhibit 10.1 lists only the 64 public institutions that could be classified in all schemes and the 30 private colleges categorized by the two schemes that included private colleges (Chapters Two and Five). The other exhibits contain every sampled college that could be classified.

Exhibit 10.1. A Comparison of Illustrative Classifications (Arranged Alphabetically by Control)

Institution	State	Katsinas (Chapter Two)	Schuyler (Chapter Three)	Cohen (Chapter Four)	Merisotis and Shedd (Chapter Five)	Shaman and Zemsky (Chapter Six)
Public Institutions						
Belleville Area College	IL	Public: suburban, multicampus	Large liberal arts	Large	Community megaconnector	Mixed focus
Belmont Technical College	OH	Public: rural, small	Small and medium	Small	Community connector	Degree focus
Bismarck State College	ND	Public: rural, small	Small and medium	Medium	Community connector	Degree focus
Cape Cod Community College	MA	Public: rural, large	Small and medium	Medium	Community connector	Course focus
Carl Sandburg College	IL	Public: rural, large	Small and medium	Small	Community connector	Mixed focus
Central Piedmont Community College	NC	Public: urban, multicampus	Large liberal arts	Large	Community megaconnector	Course focus
Chattanooga State Technical Community College	TN	Public: urban, single-campus	Large liberal arts	Large	Community megaconnector	Course focus
Chesapeake College	MD	Public: rural, small	Small and medium	Small	Community connector	Course focus
Cincinnati State Technical and Community College	OH	Public: urban, single-campus	Small and medium	Large	Community connector	Mixed focus
College of Marin	CA	Public: suburban, multicampus	Large liberal arts	Large	Community megaconnector	Course focus
Community College of Rhode Island	RI	Public: suburban, multicampus	Large liberal arts	Large	Community megaconnector	Course focus
Cuesta College	CA	Public: rural, large	Large liberal arts	Large	Community megaconnector	Mixed focus
Danville Area Community College	IL	Public: rural, large	Small and medium	Small	Community connector	Mixed focus
Eastern Iowa Community College District	IA	Public: urban, multicampus	Small and medium	Large	Community connector	Degree focus
Fayetteville Technical Community College	NC	Public: rural, large	Large liberal arts	Large	Community megaconnector	Mixed focus
Germanna Community College	VA	Public: rural, large	Small and medium	Medium	Community connector	Course focus
Hawaii Community College	HI	Public: rural, small	Small and medium	Small	Community connector	Degree focus
Helena College of Technology of University of Montana	MT	Public: rural, small	Small and medium	Small	Community development and career	Degree focus
Henry Ford Community College	MI	Public: suburban, multicampus	Large liberal arts	Large	Community megaconnector	Course focus
Hocking Technical College	OH	Public: rural, large	Small and medium	Medium	Community connector	Degree focus
Holyoke Community College	MA	Public: rural, large	Small and medium	Medium	Community connector	Mixed focus
Jefferson Davis Community College	AL	Public: rural, small	Small and medium	Small	Community connector	Degree focus
Jefferson State Community College	AL	Public: suburban, single-campus	Small and medium	Medium	Community connector	Course focus
John Wood Community College	IL	Public: rural, small	Small and medium	Small	Community connector	Degree focus
Kellogg Community College	MI	Public: rural, large	Small and medium	Medium	Community megaconnector	Degree focus

Labette Community College	KS	Public: rural, small	Small and medium	Small	Community connector	Mixed focus
Lenoir Community College	NC	Public: rural, small	Small and medium	Small	Community connector	Degree focus
Linn-Benton Community College	OR	Public: rural, large	Small and medium	Medium	Community megaconnector	Mixed focus
Lower Columbia College	WA	Public: rural, large	Small and medium	Medium	Community connector	Degree focus
Mercer County Community College	NJ	Public: suburban, multicampus	Large liberal arts	Large	Community megaconnector	Mixed focus
Metropolitan Community College Area	NE	Public: urban, multicampus	Large liberal arts	Large	Community megaconnector	Course focus
Mississippi Gulf Coast Community College	MS	Public: rural, small	Large liberal arts	Large	Community megaconnector	Mixed focus
Monroe Community College	NY	Public: urban, multicampus	Large liberal arts	Large	Community megaconnector	Degree focus
Montgomery Community College	NC	Public: rural, small	Small and medium	Small	Community development and career	Degree focus
Napa Valley College	CA	Public: suburban, single-campus	Large liberal arts	Medium	Community megaconnector	Mixed focus
Nassau Community College	NY	Public: suburban, single-campus	Large liberal arts	Large	Community megaconnector	Degree focus
New Hampshire Community Technical College-Manchester/Stratham	NH	Public: rural, large	Small and medium	Medium	Community connector	Course focus
New Hampshire Community Technical College-Nashua	NH	Public: rural, small	Small and medium	Small	Community development and career	Degree focus
New Mexico Military Institute	NM	Special-use institutions	Small and medium	Small	Community development and career	Degree focus
North Lake College	TX	Public: urban, multicampus	Small and medium	Large	Community megaconnector	Course focus
Northeastern Junior College	CO	Public: rural, large	Small and medium	Medium	Community megaconnector	Course focus
Northwestern Connecticut Community-Technical College	CT	Public: suburban, single-campus	Small and medium	Small	Community connector	Mixed focus
Norwalk Community-Technical College	CT	Public: suburban, single-campus	Small and medium	Medium	Community connector	Course focus
Oklahoma City Community College	OK	Public: urban, single-campus	Large liberal arts	Large	Community megaconnector	Course focus
Pierce College	WA	Public: suburban, single-campus	Small and medium	Large	Community megaconnector	Mixed focus
Pulaski Technical College	AR	Public: suburban, single-campus	Small and medium	Medium	Community connector	Course focus
Reid State Technical College	AL	Public: rural, small	Small and medium	Small	Community development and career	Degree focus
Rend Lake College	IL	Public: rural, large	Small and medium	Medium	Community megaconnector	Degree focus
Rock Valley College	IL	Public: rural, large	Large liberal arts	Large	Community megaconnector	Degree focus
Saint Johns River Community College	FL	Public: suburban, single-campus	Small and medium	Medium	Community connector	Course focus

Exhibit 10.1. (Continued) A Comparison of Illustrative Classifications (Arranged Alphabetically by Control)

Institution	State	Katsinas (Chapter Two)	Schuyler (Chapter Three)	Cohen (Chapter Four)	Merisotis and Shedd (Chapter Five)	Shaman and Zemsky (Chapter Six)
Southwest Mississippi Community College	MS	Public: rural, small	Small and medium	Small	Community connector	Degree focus
Southwest Virginia Community College	VA	Public: rural, large	Small and medium	Medium	Community connector	Mixed focus
Spokane Falls Community College	WA	Public: urban, multicampus	Large liberal arts	Large	Community megaconnector	Course focus
Springfield Technical Community College	MA	Public: urban, single-campus	Large liberal arts	Large	Community connector	Mixed focus
Texarkana College	TX	Public: rural, large	Small and medium	Medium	Community connector	Mixed focus
Three Rivers Community-Technical College	CT	Public: suburban, single-campus	Small and medium	Medium	Community connector	Mixed focus
Treasure Valley Community College	OR	Public: rural, small	Small and medium	Small	Community connector	Mixed focus
Trenholm State Technical College	AL	Public: rural, small	Small and medium	Small	Community development and career	Degree focus
Tri-County Technical College	SC	Public: rural, large	Small and medium	Medium	Community connector	Degree focus
Trinity Valley Community College	TX	Public: rural, large	Small and medium	Medium	Community connector	Degree focus
University of Pittsburgh-Titusville	PA	Public: rural, small	Small and medium	Small	Community development and career	Course focus
Vernon Regional Junior College	TX	Public: rural, small	Small and medium	Small	Community connector	Degree focus
Volunteer State Community College	TN	Public: rural, large	Large liberal arts	Large	Community connector	Course focus
Western Oklahoma State College	OK	Public: rural, small	Small and medium	Small	Community connector	Course focus
Private Institutions						
Cambria Rowe Business College	PA	Private, proprietary	—	—	Career connector	—
Chatfield College	OH	Private, nonprofit	—	—	Connector	—
Denver Academy of Court Reporting-Main Campus	CO	Private, proprietary	—	—	Career connector-	
ECPI College of Technology	VA	Private, proprietary	—	—	Career connector	—
Ellis Hospital School of Nursing	NY	Special-use institutions	—	—	Allied health	—
Gallipolis Career College	OH	Private, proprietary	—	—	Career connector	—
Hallmark Institute of Technology	TX	Private, proprietary	—	—	Career connector	—
Helene Fuld College of Nursing	NY	Special-use institutions	—	—	Allied health	—
Hesston College	KS	Private, nonprofit	—	—	Connector	—

Indiana Business College	IN	Private, proprietary	—	—	Career connector	—
Interboro Institute	NY	Private, proprietary	—	—	Career connector	—
ITT Technical Institute	OH	Private, proprietary	—	—	Career connector	—
ITT Technical Institute	TX	Private, proprietary	—	—	Career connector	—
Lincoln Technical Institute	PA	Private, proprietary	—	—	Career connector	—
Mary Holmes College	MS	Private, nonprofit	—	—	Connector	—
Morrison Institute of Technology	IL	Special-use institutions	—	—	Connector	—
Mountain West College-Salt Lake City	UT	Private, proprietary	—	—	Career connector	—
Newport Business Institute	PA	Private, proprietary	—	—	Career connector	—
Nielsen Electronics Institute	SC	Private, proprietary	—	—	Career connector	—
Plaza Business Institute	NY	Private, proprietary	—	—	Career connector	—
Ranken Technical College	MO	Private, nonprofit	—	—	Connector	—
Rochester Business Institute	NY	Private, proprietary	—	—	Career connector	—
Saint Catharine College	KY	Private, nonprofit	—	—	Connector	—
Southern College	FL	Private, proprietary	—	—	—	
Southwest School of Electronics	TX	Private, proprietary	—	—	Career connector	—
Spartanburg Methodist College	SC	Private, proprietary	—	—	Connector	—
Triangle Tech Incorporated-Dubois	PA	Private, proprietary	—	—	Career connector	—
Trocaire College	NY	Private, nonprofit	—	—	Connector	—
Utica School of Commerce	NY	Private, proprietary	—	—	Career connector	—
Wyoming Technical Institute	WY	Private, proprietary	—	—	Career connector	—

Note: Exhibit includes only institutions that could be classified in all relevant schemes.

Exhibit 10.2. Illustrative Classification Corresponding to Katsinas's Proposal in Chapter Two (Arranged Alphabetically by State and College Name)

I. Publicly Controlled Institutions	
Rural, Small	
Jefferson Davis Community College	AL
Reid State Technical College	AL
Trenholm State Technical College	AL
Lassen Community College	CA
Hawaii Community College	HI
John Wood Community College	IL
Ivy Tech State College-Wabash Valley	IN
Labette Community College	KS
Ashland Community College	KY
Owensboro Community College	KY
Chesapeake College	MD
Mississippi Gulf Coast Community College	MS
Southwest Mississippi Community College	MS
Helena College of Technology of University of Montana	MT
Montana State University College of Technology-Billings	MT
Montana Tech College of Technology	MT
Lenoir Community College	NC
Montgomery Community College	NC
Bismarck State College	ND
New Hampshire Community Technical College-Nashua	NH
Belmont Technical College	OH
Western Oklahoma State College	OK
Treasure Valley Community College	OR
University of Pittsburgh-Titusville	PA
Vernon Regional Junior College	TX
Rural, Large	
Cuesta College	CA
Northeastern Junior College	CO
Carl Sandburg College	IL
Danville Area Community College	IL
Rend Lake College	IL
Rock Valley College	IL
Cape Cod Community College	MA
Holyoke Community College	MA
Kellogg Community College	MI
Fayetteville Technical Community College	NC
New Hampshire Community Technical College-Manchester/Stratham	NH
University of New Mexico-Gallup Campus	NM
Hocking Technical College	OH
Linn-Benton Community College	OR
Tri-County Technical College	SC
Volunteer State Community College	TN
Texarkana College	TX
Trinity Valley Community College	TX
Germanna Community College	VA
Southwest Virginia Community College	VA
Community College of Vermont	VT
Lower Columbia College	WA

Exhibit 10.2. (Continued) Illustrative Classification Corresponding to Katsinas's Proposal in Chapter Two (Arranged Alphabetically by State and College Name)

Suburban, Single-Campus	
Jefferson State Community College	AL
Pulaski Technical College	AR
Napa Valley College	CA
Northwestern Connecticut Community-Technical College	CT
Norwalk Community-Technical College	CT
Three Rivers Community-Technical College	CT
Saint Johns River Community College	FL
Nassau Community College	NY
Pierce College	WA
Suburban, Multicampus	
College of Marin	CA
Belleville Area College	IL
Montgomery College of Germantown	MD
Henry Ford Community College	MI
Mercer County Community College	NJ
Community College of Rhode Island	RI
Urban, Single-Campus	
Ventura College	CA
Springfield Technical Community College	MA
Cincinnati State Technical And Community College	OH
Oklahoma City Community College	OK
Northampton County Area Community College	PA
Chattanooga State Technical Community College	TN
Urban, Multicampus	
Columbia College	CA
Porterville College	CA
San Diego Miramar College	CA
Eastern Iowa Community College District	IA
Dundalk Community College	MD
Central Piedmont Community College	NC
Metropolitan Community College Area	NE
Monroe Community College	NY
North Lake College	TX
Salt Lake Community College	UT
Spokane Falls Community College	WA
II. Privately Controlled Institutions	
Nonprofit	
Hesston College	KS
Saint Catharine College	KY
Ranken Technical College	MO
Mary Holmes College	MS
Trocaire College	NY
Chatfield College	OH

Exhibit 10.2. (Continued) Illustrative Classification Corresponding to Katsinas's Proposal in Chapter Two (Arranged Alphabetically by State and College Name)

Proprietary	
Heald College Schools of Business and Technology-Hayward	CA
Denver Academy of Court Reporting-Main Campus	CO
Southern College	FL
Indiana Business College	IN
Institute of Electronic Technology	KY
Mid-State College	ME
Interboro Institute	NY
Plaza Business Institute	NY
Rochester Business Institute	NY
Utica School of Commerce	NY
Gallipolis Career College	OH
ITT Technical Institute	OH
Cambria Rowe Business College	PA
Lincoln Technical Institute	PA
Newport Business Institute	PA
Triangle Tech Incorporated-Dubois	PA
Nielsen Electronics Institute	SC
Spartanburg Methodist College	SC
Hallmark Institute of Technology	TX
ITT Technical Institute	TX
Southwest School of Electronics	TX
Mountain West College-Salt Lake City	UT
ECPI College of Technology	VA
Wyoming Technical Institute	WY
III. Federally Chartered and Special-Use Institutions[a]	
Special-Use Institutions	
Morrison Institute of Technology	IL
Mid-America College of Funeral Service	IN
New Mexico Military Institute	NM
Ellis Hospital School of Nursing	NY
Helene Fuld College of Nursing	NY

[a]There were no tribal colleges in this sample.

Defining Boundaries

Ultimately, all five schemes are consistent in defining the two-year college sector with two mutually exclusive categories: public and private. Three proposals do so by excluding the private colleges altogether, while the two that include private colleges—both proprietary and nonprofit—explicitly differentiate them from the public colleges. Despite this consensus, the issue of boundaries is not entirely resolved. In Chapter Seven, Phillippe and Boggs note that the AACC definitions require that community colleges be regionally accredited. Acknowledging the importance of including the wider universe of two-year colleges, they assert that accreditation status should be an important consideration in classification. Another question of definition is illustrated by the categorization of the New Mexico Military Institute

Exhibit 10.3. Illustrative Classification Corresponding to Schuyler's Proposal in Chapter Three (Arranged Alphabetically by State and College Name)

Small and Medium	
Jefferson Davis Community College	AL
Jefferson State Community College	AL
Reid State Technical College	AL
Trenholm State Technical College	AL
Pulaski Technical College	AR
Columbia College	CA
Lassen Community College	CA
Porterville College	CA
Northeastern Junior College	CO
Northwestern Connecticut Community-Technical College	CT
Norwalk Community-Technical College	CT
Three Rivers Community-Technical College	CT
Saint Johns River Community College	FL
Hawaii Community College	HI
Eastern Iowa Community College District	IA
Carl Sandburg College	IL
Danville Area Community College	IL
John Wood Community College	IL
Rend Lake College	IL
Ivy Tech State College-Wabash Valley	IN
Labette Community College	KS
Ashland Community College	KY
Owensboro Community College	KY
Cape Cod Community College	MA
Holyoke Community College	MA
Chesapeake College	MD
Dundalk Community College	MD
Montgomery College of Germantown	MD
Kellogg Community College	MI
Southwest Mississippi Community College	MS
Helena College of Technology of University of Montana	MT
Montana State University College of Technology-Billings	MT
Montana Tech College of Technology	MT
Lenoir Community College	NC
Montgomery Community College	NC
Bismarck State College	ND
New Hampshire Community Technical College-Manchester/Stratham	NH
New Hampshire Community Technical College-Nashua	NH
New Mexico Military Institute	NM
University of New Mexico-Gallup Campus	NM
Belmont Technical College	OH
Cincinnati State Technical and Community College	OH
Hocking Technical College	OH
Western Oklahoma State College	OK
Linn-Benton Community College	OR
Treasure Valley Community College	OR
Northampton County Area Community College	PA
University of Pittsburgh-Titusville	PA
Tri-County Technical College	SC
North Lake College	TX

Exhibit 10.3. (Continued) Illustrative Classification Corresponding to Schuyler's Proposal in Chapter Three (Arranged Alphabetically by State and College Name)

Texarkana College	TX
Trinity Valley Community College	TX
Vernon Regional Junior College	TX
Germanna Community College	VA
Southwest Virginia Community College	VA
Community College of Vermont	VT
Lower Columbia College	WA
Pierce College	WA
Large Liberal Arts	
College of Marin	CA
Cuesta College	CA
Napa Valley College	CA
San Diego Miramar College	CA
Ventura College	CA
Belleville Area College	IL
Rock Valley College	IL
Springfield Technical Community College	MA
Henry Ford Community College	MI
Mississippi Gulf Coast Community College	MS
Central Piedmont Community College	NC
Fayetteville Technical Community College	NC
Metropolitan Community College Area	NE
Mercer County Community College	NJ
Monroe Community College	NY
Nassau Community College	NY
Oklahoma City Community College	OK
Community College of Rhode Island	RI
Chattanooga State Technical Community College	TN
Volunteer State Community College	TN
Salt Lake Community College	UT
Spokane Falls Community College	WA

(NMMI). Katsinas's model identifies NMMI as a "special-use institution," although in the rest of the models NMMI is grouped with other public colleges. Katsinas's separation of NMMI from the rest of the public colleges in the sample raises questions of whether, or in what ways, NMMI and similar institutions are comparable to the other public colleges.

Phillippe and Boggs suggest an additional way of approaching the public-private divide. They contend that classification by organizational structure is especially useful for state-level policymaking, but not in isolation from categorization based on colleges' curricular or programmatic offerings. Programmatic categories, they assert, could help distinguish the colleges within the "special-use" class. Indeed, perhaps a consideration of the instructional programs at private colleges could inform the instructional classification of public ones. As Shaman and Zemsky suggest in their

Exhibit 10.4. Illustrative Classification Corresponding to Cohen's Proposal in Chapter Four (Arranged Alphabetically by State and College Name)

Small	
Jefferson Davis Community College	AL
Reid State Technical College	AL
Trenholm State Technical College	AL
Northwestern Connecticut Community-Technical College	CT
Hawaii Community College	HI
Carl Sandburg College	IL
Danville Area Community College	IL
John Wood Community College	IL
Ivy Tech State College-Wabash Valley	IN
Labette Community College	KS
Chesapeake College	MD
Southwest Mississippi Community College	MS
Helena College of Technology of University of Montana	MT
Lenoir Community College	NC
Montgomery Community College	NC
New Hampshire Community Technical College-Nashua	NH
New Mexico Military Institute	NM
University of New Mexico-Gallup Campus	NM
Belmont Technical College	OH
Western Oklahoma State College	OK
Treasure Valley Community College	OR
University of Pittsburgh-Titusville	PA
Vernon Regional Junior College	TX
Medium	
Jefferson State Community College	AL
Pulaski Technical College	AR
Napa Valley College	CA
Northeastern Junior College	CO
Norwalk Community-Technical College	CT
Three Rivers Community-Technical College	CT
Saint Johns River Community College	FL
Rend Lake College	IL
Cape Cod Community College	MA
Holyoke Community College	MA
Kellogg Community College	MI
Bismarck State College	ND
New Hampshire Community Technical College-Manchester/Stratham	NH
Hocking Technical College	OH
Linn-Benton Community College	OR
Northampton County Area Community College	PA
Tri-County Technical College	SC
Texarkana College	TX
Trinity Valley Community College	TX
Germanna Community College	VA
Southwest Virginia Community College	VA
Community College of Vermont	VT
Lower Columbia College	WA

Exhibit 10.4. (Continued) Illustrative Classification Corresponding to Cohen's Proposal in Chapter Four (Arranged Alphabetically by State and College Name)

Large	
College of Marin	CA
Cuesta College	CA
Ventura College	CA
Eastern Iowa Community College District	IA
Belleville Area College	IL
Rock Valley College	IL
Springfield Technical Community College	MA
Henry Ford Community College	MI
Mississippi Gulf Coast Community College	MS
Central Piedmont Community College	NC
Fayetteville Technical Community College	NC
Metropolitan Community College Area	NE
Mercer County Community College	NJ
Monroe Community College	NY
Nassau Community College	NY
Cincinnati State Technical and Community College	OH
Oklahoma City Community College	OK
Community College of Rhode Island	RI
Chattanooga State Technical Community College	TN
Volunteer State Community College	TN
North Lake College	TX
Salt Lake Community College	UT
Pierce College	WA
Spokane Falls Community College	WA

analysis, the two-year educational market encompasses multiple instructional services, blurring the lines between credit and noncredit or academic and occupational.

Functional Differences Among Classifications

Despite their shared focus on distinguishing colleges by enrollment and related characteristics, the proposals in Chapters Three through Six have discrepant results when applied to the sample. For example, Cohen notes the importance of the curriculum in distinguishing community colleges, reiterating Schuyler's finding that the higher the enrollment, the larger the proportion of classes in the traditional liberal arts. This holds true for most, but not all, of the colleges sampled for this project. Four colleges designated as "large" colleges in terms of enrollment (Chapter Four) are not part of the "large liberal arts" category (Chapter Three). What are the practical implications for Eastern Iowa Community College District, Cincinnati State Technical and Community College, North Lake College, and Pierce College? Do these four exceptions indicate a need for more precise categories?

Exhibit 10.5. Illustrative Classification Corresponding to Merisotis and Shedd's Proposal in Chapter Five (Arranged Alphabetically by State and College Name)

Community Development and Career Institutions	
Reid State Technical College	AL
Trenholm State Technical College	AL
Helena College of Technology of University of Montana	MT
Montgomery Community College	NC
New Hampshire Community Technical College-Nashua	NH
New Mexico Military Institute	NM
University of Pittsburgh-Titusville	PA
Community Connector Institutions	
Jefferson Davis Community College	AL
Jefferson State Community College	AL
Pulaski Technical College	AR
Lassen Community College	CA
Porterville College	CA
Northwestern Connecticut Community-Technical College	CT
Norwalk Community-Technical College	CT
Three Rivers Community-Technical College	CT
Saint Johns River Community College	FL
Hawaii Community College	HI
Eastern Iowa Community College District	IA
Carl Sandburg College	IL
Danville Area Community College	IL
John Wood Community College	IL
Labette Community College	KS
Cape Cod Community College	MA
Holyoke Community College	MA
Springfield Technical Community College	MA
Chesapeake College	MD
Dundalk Community College	MD
Southwest Mississippi Community College	MS
Lenoir Community College	NC
Bismarck State College	ND
New Hampshire Community Technical College-Manchester/Stratham	NH
Belmont Technical College	OH
Cincinnati State Technical and Community College	OH
Hocking Technical College	OH
Western Oklahoma State College	OK
Treasure Valley Community College	OR
Tri-County Technical College	SC
Volunteer State Community College	TN
Texarkana College	TX
Trinity Valley Community College	TX
Vernon Regional Junior College	TX
Germanna Community College	VA
Southwest Virginia Community College	VA
Lower Columbia College	WA

Exhibit 10.5. (Continued) Illustrative Classification Corresponding to Merisotis and Shedd's Proposal in Chapter Five (Arranged Alphabetically by State and College Name)

Community Megaconnector Institutions	
College of Marin	CA
Cuesta College	CA
Napa Valley College	CA
Northeastern Junior College	CO
Belleville Area College	IL
Rend Lake College	IL
Rock Valley College	IL
Henry Ford Community College	MI
Kellogg Community College	MI
Mississippi Gulf Coast Community College	MS
Central Piedmont Community College	NC
Fayetteville Technical Community College	NC
Metropolitan Community College Area	NE
Mercer County Community College	NJ
Monroe Community College	NY
Nassau Community College	NY
Oklahoma City Community College	OK
Linn-Benton Community College	OR
Community College of Rhode Island	RI
Chattanooga State Technical Community College	TN
North Lake College	TX
Pierce College	WA
Spokane Falls Community College	WA
Allied Health Institutions	
Ellis Hospital School of Nursing	NY
Helene Fuld College of Nursing	NY
Connector Institutions	
Morrison Institute of Technology	IL
Hesston College	KS
Saint Catharine College	KY
Ranken Technical College	MO
Mary Holmes College	MS
Trocaire College	NY
Chatfield College	OH
Spartanburg Methodist College	SC
Career Connector Institutions	
Denver Academy of Court Reporting-Main Campus	CO
Southern College	FL
Indiana Business College	IN
Interboro Institute	NY
Plaza Business Institute	NY
Rochester Business Institute	NY
Utica School of Commerce	NY
ITT Technical Institute	OH
Gallipolis Career College	OH
Cambria Rowe Business College	PA

Exhibit 10.5. (Continued) Illustrative Classification Corresponding to Merisotis and Shedd's Proposal in Chapter Five (Arranged Alphabetically by State and College Name)

Lincoln Technical Institute	PA
Newport Business Institute	PA
Triangle Tech Incorporated-Dubois	PA
Nielsen Electronics Institute	SC
Hallmark Institute of Technology	TX
ITT Technical Institute	TX
Southwest School of Electronics	TX
Mountain West College-Salt Lake City	UT
ECPI College of Technology	VA
Wyoming Technical Institute	WY

Note: There were no certificate institutions in this sample.

Furthermore, comparison of Schuyler's proposal with Shaman and Zemsky's reveals distinct variance between the two conceptual approaches. For instance, of the eighteen colleges designated "large liberal arts" by Schuyler, eight are "course focus" colleges, seven are "mixed," and three are "degree focus," according to Shaman and Zemsky. A similar divergence appears in Merisotis and Shedd's approach.

Such differences in grouping patterns may be analytically instructive. Conversely, they may simply cause confusion. In examining the exhibits in this chapter, one reviewer noted that the classification of Fayetteville Technical Community College among "large liberal arts" colleges (Chapter Three) is entirely inconsistent with its statutory mission and would likely cause considerable consternation among its institutional or system leaders. This observation calls attention to the limitations of classification according to empirical criteria that substitute for the phenomenon of genuine interest. The classification serves as a simplification, but as Schuyler found, this can result in misclassifications in either direction (what in other applications might be called false positives and false negatives). One implication is that classification should not be confused with identity, nor should more authority be attributed to it than is justified by the underlying methodology. Thus classification according to site visits and intensive analysis—while not practical for a comprehensive classification—might justifiably claim greater authority.

However, examining each scheme simply to uncover contradictions is not particularly constructive. As Cohen notes, it is very likely that any *single* classification scheme will be deemed inadequate by community college stakeholders. In fact, none of the proposed classifications meet the full set of assessment criteria outlined in de los Santos's commentary. These categories do not offer nuanced descriptions of individual colleges; rather they function as heuristics for thinking about the entire landscape of two-year colleges. At this preliminary stage, the differences among these classifications and the

Exhibit 10.6. Illustrative Classification Corresponding to Shaman and Zemsky's Proposal in Chapter Six (Arranged Alphabetically by State and College Name)

Degree Focus	
Jefferson Davis Community College	AL
Reid State Technical College	AL
Trenholm State Technical College	AL
Lassen Community College	CA
Hawaii Community College	HI
Eastern Iowa Community College District	IA
John Wood Community College	IL
Rend Lake College	IL
Rock Valley College	IL
Kellogg Community College	MI
Southwest Mississippi Community College	MS
Helena College of Technology of University of Montana	MT
Montana Tech College of Technology	MT
Lenoir Community College	NC
Montgomery Community College	NC
Bismarck State College	ND
New Hampshire Community Technical College-Nashua	NH
New Mexico Military Institute	NM
Monroe Community College	NY
Nassau Community College	NY
Belmont Technical College	OH
Hocking Technical College	OH
Northampton County Area Community College	PA
Tri-County Technical College	SC
Trinity Valley Community College	TX
Vernon Regional Junior College	TX
Lower Columbia College	WA
Mixed Focus	
Columbia College	CA
Cuesta College	CA
Napa Valley College	CA
Northwestern Connecticut Community-Technical College	CT
Three Rivers Community-Technical College	CT
Belleville Area College	IL
Carl Sandburg College	IL
Danville Area Community College	IL
Ivy Tech State College-Wabash Valley	IN
Labette Community College	KS
Owensboro Community College	KY
Holyoke Community College	MA
Springfield Technical Community College	MA
Mississippi Gulf Coast Community College	MS
Fayetteville Technical Community College	NC
Mercer County Community College	NJ
Cincinnati State Technical and Community College	OH
Linn-Benton Community College	OR
Treasure Valley Community College	OR

Exhibit 10.6. (Continued) Illustrative Classification Corresponding to Shaman and Zemsky's Proposal in Chapter Six (Arranged Alphabetically by State and College Name)

Texarkana College	TX
Salt Lake Community College	UT
Southwest Virginia Community College	VA
Pierce College	WA
Course Focus	
Jefferson State Community College	AL
Pulaski Technical College	AR
College of Marin	CA
Porterville College	CA
San Diego Miramar College	CA
Ventura College	CA
Northeastern Junior College	CO
Norwalk Community-Technical College	CT
Saint Johns River Community College	FL
Ashland Community College	KY
Cape Cod Community College	MA
Chesapeake College	MD
Dundalk Community College	MD
Montgomery College of Germantown	MD
Henry Ford Community College	MI
Central Piedmont Community College	NC
Metropolitan Community College Area	NE
New Hampshire Community Technical College-Manchester/Stratham	NH
University of New Mexico-Gallup Campus	NM
Oklahoma City Community College	OK
Western Oklahoma State College	OK
University of Pittsburgh-Titusville	PA
Community College of Rhode Island	RI
Chattanooga State Technical Community College	TN
Volunteer State Community College	TN
North Lake College	TX
Germanna Community College	VA
Community College of Vermont	VT
Spokane Falls Community College	WA

patterns that emerge across schemes are important because they offer a foundation for the next iteration of the classification discussion.

Consider, for example, Shaman and Zemsky's "degree focus" classification. Within the sample of colleges selected for this volume, the size of the degree focus colleges varies: in Cohen's classification, eleven are "small," seven are "medium," and four are "large." A more telling pattern, however, arises from applying Katsinas's categories. With the exception of five colleges in this sample, the "degree focus" colleges correspond to a single geographical designation: "rural." Is there something to be gained from this information—either about "degree focus" colleges or "rural" colleges?

Unfortunately, the most significant implications of this practical exercise are revealed by absences. Each classification is presented and critiqued with a fundamental caveat: adequate classification is severely compromised by the data currently available. In some instances, the goal of each classification scheme and the proxies relied on to circumvent the gaps in data are not tightly linked.

Even seemingly straightforward categories, such as rural, urban, or suburban setting, present complications. Katsinas mentions a few when explaining how he identified colleges serving "the urban core" of metropolitan areas, thereby distinguishing between urban and suburban colleges. Fundamentally, this is an issue of demographics—not only of each college's service area but also of the college's student population. In reporting findings from a large-scale study of community colleges, Vanessa Smith Morest (2003) describes two contrasting types of "urban" colleges. Her comparison of racial demographics of the community with those of the student population revealed that some colleges have a substantially greater proportion of white students enrolled than live in the surrounding area. Alternatively, in other colleges the pattern is reversed. Additional factors distinguish these "urban" colleges, including different access to resources and relationships to nearby four-year colleges. As a result, these two types of "urban" community colleges differ in multiple, significant ways. While Katsinas recognizes the differences among urban colleges and attempts to limit the definition to colleges that serve the "core" of America's central cities, his parameters do not address the interrelated matrix of demographics, funding, and four-year college proximity.

Even the potential simplicity of classification by size obscures the range of variation among two-year colleges. Although the cut-off numbers for small, medium, and large colleges used in the classification proposals create groups of roughly equal size, these three categories may need refinement. In particular, the "large" category encompasses colleges with student enrollments from 7,000 to nearly 30,000.

Every author included in this volume has noted shortcomings in the available data. The most often cited concerns include the need for adequate information on curricular offerings, including noncredit courses; funding structures, such as formulas for state and local appropriations; and characteristics of the communities that two-year colleges serve.

Indeed, the role of local contexts in shaping community colleges' missions, structures, and outcomes demands a more sophisticated database at the national level. In this regard, it is worth reiterating Bailey's remark, that if the classification process were to result in the collection of currently inaccessible data, "the process would represent a significant advance for research."

The movement to establish classification schemes for two-year colleges is in its infancy. The classification models assembled in this volume illustrate a range of possible approaches to the problem, each with strengths and weaknesses. The insights generated by the contributors offer an informed basis for the next stage of conceptualizing and refining the classification of two-year colleges.

Reference

Morest, V. S. *Community College Missions.* New York: Community College Research Center, Teachers College, Columbia University, 2003.

REBECCA D. COX is a Ph.D. candidate in education at the University of California, Berkeley.

ALEXANDER C. MCCORMICK is a senior scholar at The Carnegie Foundation for the Advancement of Teaching, where he directs the Carnegie Classification of Institutions of Higher Education.

INDEX

Back Issue/Subscription Order Form

Copy or detach and send to:
Jossey-Bass, A Wiley Company, 989 Market Street, San Francisco CA 94103-1741

Call or fax toll-free: Phone 888-378-2537 6:30AM – 3PM PST; Fax 888-481-2665

Back Issues: Please send me the following issues at $28 each
(Important: please include ISBN number with your order.)

____

____

____

$ __________ Total for single issues

$ __________ SHIPPING CHARGES: SURFACE

	Domestic	Canadian
First Item	$5.00	$6.00
Each Add'l Item	$3.00	$1.50

For next-day and second-day delivery rates, call the number listed above.

Subscriptions Please __ start __ renew my subscription to *New Directions for Community Colleges* for the year 2____at the following rate:

U.S.	__ Individual $70	__ Institutional $149
Canada	__ Individual $70	__ Institutional $189
All Others	__ Individual $94	__ Institutional $223
Online Subscription		__ Institutional $149

For more information about online subscriptions visit www.interscience.wiley.com

$ __________ Total single issues and subscriptions (Add appropriate sales tax for your state for single issue orders. No sales tax for U.S. subscriptions. Canadian residents, add GST for subscriptions and single issues.)

__Payment enclosed (U.S. check or money order only)
__VISA __ MC __ AmEx __ # ________________________Exp. Date ______

Signature ______________________________ Day Phone ____________
__ Bill Me (U.S. institutional orders only. Purchase order required.)

Purchase order # ____

Federal Tax ID 13559302 **GST 09102 8052**

Name ____

Address ____

____

Phone ________________________ E-mail __________________________

For more information about Jossey-Bass, visit our Web site at www.josseybass.com

PROMOTION CODE ND03

Other Titles Available in the New Directions for Community Colleges Series

Arthur M. Cohen, Editor-in-Chief
Florence B. Brawer, Associate Editor

CC121 **The Role of the Community College in Teacher Education**
Barbara K. Townsend, Jan M. Ignash
Illustrates the extent to which community colleges have become major players in teacher education, not only in the traditional way of providing the first two years of an undergraduate degree in teacher education but in more controversial ways such as offering associate and baccalaureate degrees in teacher education and providing alternative certification programs.
ISBN: 0-7879-6868-4

CC120 **Enhancing Community Colleges Through Professional Development**
Gordon E. Watts
Offers a much needed perspective on the expanding role of professional development in community colleges. Chapter authors provide descriptions of how their institutions have addressed issues through professional development, created institutional change, developed new delivery systems for professional development, reached beyond development just for faculty, and found new uses for traditional development activities.
ISBN: 0-7879-6330-5

CC119 **Developing Successful Partnerships with Business and the Community**
Mary S. Spangler
Demonstrates that there are many different approaches to community colleges' partnering with the private sector and that when partners are actively engaged in tailoring education, training, and learning to their students, everyone is the beneficiary.
ISBN: 0-7879-6321-9

CC118 **Community College Faculty: Characteristics, Practices, and Challenges**
Charles Outcalt
Offers multiple perspectives on the ways community college faculty fulfill their complex professional roles. With data from national surveys, this volume provides an overview of community college faculty, looks at their primary teaching responsibility, and examines particular groups of instructors, including part-timers, women, and people of color.
ISBN: 0-7879-6328-3

CC117 **Next Steps for the Community College**
Trudy H. Bers, Harriott D. Calhoun
Provides an overview of relevant literature and practice covering major community college topics: transfer rates, vocational education, remedial and developmental education, English as a second language education, assessment of student learning, student services, faculty and staff, and governance and policy. Includes a chapter discussing the categories, types, and purposes of literature about community colleges and the major publications germane to community college practitioners and scholars.
ISBN: 0-7879-6289-9

CC116 **The Community College Role in Welfare to Work**
C. David Lisman
Provides examples of effective programs including a job placement program meeting the needs of rural welfare recipients, short-term and advanced levels of technical training, a call center program for customer service job training, beneficial postsecondary training, collaborative programs for long-term family economic self-sufficiency, and a family-based approach recognizing the needs of welfare recipients and their families.
ISBN: 0-7879-5781-X

CC115 **The New Vocationalism in Community Colleges**
Debra D. Bragg
Analyzes the role of community college leaders in developing programs, successful partnerships and collaboration with communities, work-based learning, changes in perception of terminal education and transfer education, changing instructional practices for changing student populations and the integration of vocational education into the broader agenda of American higher education.
ISBN: 0-7879-5780-1

CC114 **Transfer Students: Trends and Issues**
Frankie Santos Laanan
Evaluates recent research and policy discussions surrounding transfer students, and summarizes three broad themes in transfer policy: research, student and academic issues, and institutional factors. Argues that institutions are in a strategic position to provide students with programs for rigorous academic training as well as opportunities to participate in formal articulation agreements with senior institutions.
ISBN: 0-7879-5779-8

CC113 **Systems for Offering Concurrent Enrollment at High Schools and Community Colleges**
Piedad F. Robertson, Brian G. Chapman, Fred Gaskin
Offers approaches to creating valuable programs, detailing all the components necessary for the success and credibility of concurrent enrollment. Focuses on the faculty liaisons from appropriate disciplines that provide the framework for an ever-improving program.
ISBN: 0-7879-5758-5

CC112 **Beyond Access: Methods and Models for Increasing Retention and Learning Among Minority Students**
Steven R. Aragon
Presents practical models, alternative approaches, and new strategies for creating effective cross-cultural courses that foster higher retention and learning success for minority students. Argues that educational programs must now develop a broader curriculum that includes multicultural and multi-linguistic information.
ISBN: 0-7879-5429-2

NEW DIRECTIONS FOR COMMUNITY COLLEGES IS NOW AVAILABLE ONLINE AT WILEY INTERSCIENCE

What is Wiley InterScience?

Wiley InterScience is the dynamic online content service from John Wiley & Sons delivering the full text of over 300 leading scientific, technical, medical, and professional journals, plus major reference works, the acclaimed *Current Protocols* laboratory manuals, and even the full text of select Wiley print books online.

What are some special features of Wiley InterScience?

Wiley InterScience Alerts is a service that delivers table of contents via e-mail for any journal available on Wiley InterScience as soon as a new issue is published online.
Early View is Wiley's exclusive service presenting individual articles online as soon as they are ready, even before the release of the compiled print issue. These articles are complete, peer-reviewed, and citable.
CrossRef is the innovative multi-publisher reference linking system enabling readers to move seamlessly from a reference in a journal article to the cited publication, typically located on a different server and published by a different publisher.

How can I access Wiley InterScience?

Visit http://www.interscience.wiley.com

Guest Users can browse Wiley InterScience for unrestricted access to journal Tables of Contents and Article Abstracts, or use the powerful search engine.
Registered Users are provided with a *Personal Home Page* to store and manage customized alerts, searches, and links to favorite journals and articles. Additionally, Registered Users can view free Online Sample Issues and preview selected material from major reference works.
Licensed Customers are entitled to access full-text journal articles in PDF, with select journals also offering full-text HTML.

How do I become an Authorized User?

Authorized Users are individuals authorized by a paying Customer to have access to the journals in Wiley InterScience. For example, a university that subscribes to Wiley journals is considered to be the Customer. Faculty, staff and students authorized by the university to have access to those journals in Wiley InterScience are Authorized Users. Users should contact their Library for information on which Wiley journals they have access to in Wiley InterScience.

ASK YOUR INSTITUTION ABOUT WILEY INTERSCIENCE TODAY!